A Message from

Ageless Glamour Girls has blessed me! I appreciated and found myself in each story. Marqueeta Curtis-Haynes, your ability to recognize a need, have compassion, bring people together, initiate a plan, and give it life has inspired me more than I can say! Thank you for loving and embracing us, Ageless Glamour Girls! You and each co-author painted such vivid pictures. I was there in each story – I cried, laughed, hoped, and prayed with you.

Thank you all for sharing your truth and helping me remember, recognize my healing, embrace my tears, dance harder, declare glory, rediscover, and sharpen the skills in my toolbox, know my worth, see my beauty at 56 years, and love and own the *ageless glamour girl* I am!

Now, more than ever, I realize that the power of family and community is vital to continuing peacefully and healthy in these aging years. Its strength is immeasurable, its reach is endless, and the need is overwhelming.

The AGG movement has and will transform many lives! I look forward with great anticipation to the next wave of glory. I pray blessings upon AGG's success!

Phyllis M. Bridges
HarvestSeed Collective, LLC.

To LaVon,
Thank you!
Enjoy!
CR Featherson

FOREWORD By Pat Battle, News Anchor/Journalist

AGELESS
Glamour Girls™
REFLECTIONS ON AGING
Bold. Beautiful. Brilliant.

MARQUEETA CURTIS-HAYNES
with 12 Co-Authors

HOV
PUBLISHING

AGELESS Glamour Girls™:
Reflections on Aging

Copyright ©2023 by Marqueeta Curtis-Haynes

All rights reserved. No part of this book may be reproduced, copied, stored, or transmitted in any form or by any means – graphic, electronic, or mechanical, including photocopying, recording, or information storage and retrieval systems without the prior written permission of Marqueeta Curtis-Haynes except where permitted by law.

HOV Publishing is a division of HOV, LLC.
www.90daybookcreation.com
hopeofvision@gmail.com

Cover Design: HOV Design Solutions
Editor: Phyllis Bridges for HarvestSeed Collective, LLC.

Marqueeta Curtis-Haynes
Ageless Glamour Girls™
Email: info@agelessglamourgirls.com
www.agelessglamourgirls.com

For further information regarding special discounts on bulk purchases, please contact: Marqueeta Curtis-Haynes at info@agelessglamourgirls.com

ISBN Paperback: 978-1-955107-44-0
ISBN eBook: 978-1-955107-43-3

Printed in the United States of America

Dedication

I dedicate this book to Ageless Glamour Girls™ around the world. I am grateful to those who shared their expertise, wisdom, and personal stories for the Ageless Glamour Girls™ brand, and to all who have supported my vision. This amazing group includes my husband, Jerry; my sister Marsha; my brother 'Dino'; my niece Maya Lynn; my stepchildren Amber and Charles; and my late mother-in-law, Bobbie Haynes. Also, my late grandmother, Ruby 'Mama Ruby' Scott, the quintessential Ageless Glamour Girl, who taught me the invaluable lesson that true beauty doesn't require even a hint of makeup.

Lastly, I dedicate this book to my late parents, Millard and Audrey Curtis, especially my mother, who was always determined to shape me into a lady of substance and class. Her dedication was the driving force behind 'Ageless Glamour Girls™'. Thank you, Mom!

Thanks to all! Xoxoxoxoxoxo

Acknowledgments

Chapter 1: The Birth of Ageless Glamour Girls™
Marqueeta Curtis-Haynes

I am deeply thankful to many, starting with God and of course – YOU – the wonderful "Ageless" community – THANK-YOU! Thanks to the strangers I've met along the way, who rooted for me after I told them about my Ageless Glamour Girls™ brand. To Ageless Glamour Girls around the world, who are ignoring the status quo, disrupting aging, and living their best ageless lives vibrantly, we've got this! And a special thanks to my fierce Sorors of Delta Sigma Theta Sorority, Inc.!

Words can't describe my feelings for my amazing co-authors, who believed in me and joined me on this journey. I am forever grateful. I love you ladies! I can't thank my publisher enough, Germaine Miller-Summers of HOV Publishing for her expertise and belief in me and the Ageless Glamour Girls™ vision. And for reaching out to me to do this wonderful anthology. I so appreciate you!

I am thankful for my dear friend, Pat Battle, for always telling me the real deal and giving me so many gut-wrenching laughs; my friend Charles Williams of WEG Media, for your constant nudging and helping to make my podcast hum; my friend and co-author, Maria Gonzalez, for your friendship and unwavering support throughout the *entire* AGG journey. A huge shout-out to my other ageless sisters in my circle, my cheering squad! I love you guys!

To my husband, Jerry D. Haynes, your love, support, humor, and guidance mean the world to me. I love you! To my wonderful siblings, Marsha Curtis-Jones and Millard "Dino" Curtis Jr., and their families – John, Anita, Millard James, Maya Lynn, and Kennedi Audrey, I love you all! And a special thanks to my stepchildren, Amber Haynes Winn, (and husband Mike), and Charles Haynes. I love you, and I'm so thankful to be your Bonus Mom.

Lastly, I am eternally grateful to my late parents, who unknowingly sowed the seeds for Ageless Glamour Girls™ and much more. Thank you, until we meet again…

Xoxoxoxo

Chapter 2: Aging My Way
Sandi Badash

I thank Hollywood for now making movies that star older, still very talented actresses who were previously put on the shelf as romantic leads. On the other hand, politics is still threatened by our strengths! I'm so proud of who aging women are and have always been: intelligent, strong, and experienced!

On a personal note, I thank the women in my life who exemplify the best of today's independence. My esteem goes to my daughter, Lisa; my daughter-in-law, Vicky; my friends, Mayra, Bernice, and Cheryl; and my cousins, Jan and Lynn. I'm proud of you all!

Chapter 3: Finding Joy
Melinda Rinzivillo

Thank you to my mother for the endless hours she spent listening to every paper, essay, poem, and story I ever wrote. To my college English professor, Sister Eileen McMahon, who taught me how to write. She pushed me, critiqued me, supported me, and challenged me to write stories from the depths of my heart; Angela Black, psychic medium, who upon our very first meeting, channeled my beloved first-born nephew, Brian, who encouraged me to do what I always wanted to do, and get on with the business of writing and sharing my stories. And especially to God the Father, for uplifting me and guiding me to find my joy. I am forever grateful…

Chapter 4: The Antidote to Aging is Belonging
Karen Herlands

I am so thankful to my dear friends, Nancy Winslow-Keane, Nanci Welsch, Donna Schneider, Thelma Molina, and my sister, Amy Eisenberg, who fill my life with laughter and wisdom. They have taught me that even in our later "ageless aging" years, it's never too late to make a new friend and share a few stories.

And to my husband, Ross, and children, Liza and Jared, I cherish you and thank you for showing me the real meaning of family.

Chapter 5: Choosing Healthspan and not just Lifespan
Ciriaca Yolanda Sabio

I am so honored to be a part of this collaboration of Ageless Glamour Girls! It has been such a great opportunity for us to tell our unique story. I know it will bless, enlighten, and make the reader laugh and smile because, as the song says, "We Are Every Woman!"

Thank you, Marqueeta, for your vision, Germaine, for your publishing expertise, and my fellow co-authors for coming together for this very important endeavor.

Chapter 6: On Second and Third Acts: Pull Out Your Transferable Skills Toolbox
Lisa Bedian

In memory of my late grandparents, Armenian Genocide survivors whose DNA gave me strength, resilience and courage; my parents, Aunt Mary, Aunt Corky, and Uncle George; my mentors, and coaches who set examples and high expectations for me; my lifelong best friend, Melanie,

40+ year friend and editor Susie, more friends than I deserve, and my Alpha Sigma Alpha, Alpha Beta chapter sisters, your support and encouragement through all my crazy adventures and career transitions have been a source of strength and inspiration. And, to my amazing husband, Bob, you bring joy, love, and fun to my life every day. I couldn't do it without you!

Chapter 7: The Unicorn: A Journey of Grace, Healing, and Rarity

Dionne Jones

I know this journey was meant to bring me to my purpose in life and for that I am truly grateful. The Universe has guided me along the way while strategically placing Earth Angels in my path. Firstly, thank you to my parents and siblings for coming along on this healing journey with me. Many families don't want to heal or don't know how to heal. Thank you to my family, as the healing process is ongoing, but we know it is well worth the fight.

The Dressler Crew, you already know! Mad love, always! Lastly, my rock, I will be forever indebted to the Universe for aligning our paths, as you showed me what healthy and flourishing love could be and is! Thank you for being a phenomenal Poppa Bear to our 2 sons and a great man. Love you!

Chapter 8: You Are Not Alone: Dealing with Grief and Loss

Lynn Venhaus

These past five years have been a difficult journey of insight, connection, and comfort. I am grateful to my sisters, Julie Modde and Mary Clare Gastro, and their spouses, Dean and Ken – "We are Zipfel Strong!", my son, Charlie Venhaus, and his wife, Maria and her Gencev family, his dad, Bob Venhaus and family, my dearest friends and family members, and the many people in Tim's life who loved him so much. Because we knew him, we have been changed for good and will forever share that bond.

Chapter 9: My Grand Journey
Cheryl Collier

I am thankful to Marqueeta for helping me become an Ageless Glamour Girl. To my husband, Barry, for always supporting everything I do, to my daughters, and son and his wife, you are loved. And to my grands, Da Boo, Jacey, Mase, Madds, and C.K. for being awesome.

Chapter 10: Life Lessons and Observations of a Mother
Maria Gonzalez

I thank Ageless Glamour Girl, Marqueeta Curtis-Haynes, for years of friendship and laughter as we travel this aging journey. To my children, Douglas, Kyle, David, Cheyenne, and my husband, Douglas, thank you for the platinum hair and thrills of being both a parent and spouse. I love you all to the moon and back! And a special welcome to the newest member of my family, daughter Bhavika. Much love to my council of women. Your words of wisdom, advice, and encouragement have been the fuel that kept my light shining even in the darkest of times. Love to my parents, my sissy

Antoinette and those relatives and friends that have gone to the next plane of existence. GOD, thank you for everything!

Chapter 11: Butterflies

Marian R. Featherson

I am so blessed, and I give honor and praise! Thanks to each of you for exhibiting strength, beauty, class, and elegance in every stage of life. With love and respect to my mother, Mrs. Earlene G. Saffore, my mother-in-law, the late Mrs. Ruth Ann Featherson, my stepmother, the late Mrs. Lula Mae Sykes, and my grandmother, the late Mrs. Mary Alice Nance. To my elders: Mrs. Vatarine Jackson Smith, Ms. Julia Lucas, and aunties, Ms. Marion Featherson, and Ms. Janet Parks. To my Prayer Warrior, Rev. Dr. Evette Loper Watt. To my husband, Vincent, our children, and goddaughter. To my sisters, brothers, family, and friends, I am forever grateful to each of you for your love and support! Thank you all for being a part of God's perfect plan.

Chapter 12: A Golden Life
Patricia Desamours

Family is everything and I would like to thank my family for the love and support they give me unconditionally. My daughter, Brittany, is the light of my life. She always encourages me to keep pushing, even when I do not believe I can. My dad, Oscar and my sister Ann are constant sources of strength for me. They love me unconditionally and that is a rare gift. Also, a big thank you to my friends. If you are my friend, I consider you part of my family. I appreciate your constant encouragement and love. With all that positive reinforcement from family and friends, I embrace each day, and life keeps getting better.

Chapter 13: Sweet Inspiration
Leah Irene Victoria

I would like to thank Marqueeta Curtis-Haynes for giving me the opportunity to be a part of this incredible project and those individuals who believed in my ability to impact others positively.

While on this journey, there have been people that have come into my life and influenced me tremendously such as my parents, siblings, and extended family members. Then there are those who served their purpose during their brief but inspirational stay such as my teachers, mentors, and a number of doctors who have shaped me and guided me professionally up to now. This chapter is dedicated to them, and this is why I call this chapter, "Sweet Inspiration."

Table of Contents

Foreword — xxi

Preface — xxv

Chapter 1: The Birth of Ageless Glamour Girls™ — 1
Marqueeta Curtis-Haynes

Chapter 2: Aging My Way — 17
Sandi Badash

Chapter 3: Finding My Joy — 25
Melinda Rinzivillo

Chapter 4: The Antidote to Aging is Belonging — 35
Karen Herlands

Chapter 5: Choosing Healthspan and Not Just Lifespan — 45
Ciriaca Yolanda Sabio

Chapter 6: On Second and Third Acts: Pull Out Your Transferable Skills Toolbox — 61
Lisa Bedian

Chapter 7: The Unicorn: A Journey of Grace, Healing, and Rarity   71
Dionne Jones

Chapter 8: You Are Not Alone: Dealing with Grief and Loss   85
Lynn Venhaus

Chapter 9: My Grand Journey   107
Cheryl Collier

Chapter 10: Life Lessons and Observations of a Mother   117
Maria Gonzalez

Chapter 11: Butterflies   137
Marian R. Featherson

Chapter 12: A Golden Life   151
Patricia Desamours

Chapter 13: Sweet Inspirations   163
Leah Irene Victoria

Epilogue: Pat Battle   169

About Ageless Glamour Girls™   173

Foreword

Written by Pat Battle, News Anchor/Journalist

I have been blessed to spend more than 40 years as a working journalist in newspaper and television. So, you can imagine I have written and read more words, met, and spoken to more people than I can count. I am fast approaching my 30th year as an anchor and reporter for WNBC-TV in New York, the flagship station of NBC's owned and operated local news division. My career has taken me from my first job as a print reporter at the Asbury Park Press, New Jersey's third-largest newspaper, to my first TV job at the state's public television station, New Jersey Nightly, to the City of Brotherly Love and my first foray into commercial television news as a reporter and host at WCAU-TV, the CBS "O & O" in Philadelphia.

When my contract wasn't renewed, I thought my career in television news may have ended there. I know now it was all part of a bigger plan. I was hired by WCBS-TV, the network's flagship station in New York City, in 1992. I walked into the newsroom and was met by a smiling, red-lipstick-wearing ball of energy and enthusiasm. With arms wide open for a hug, she introduced herself as Marqueeta. That smile launched a 40-year friendship that I am blessed to say endures today. Marqueeta was a gifted news writer, but her talent and passion is bringing women together. We would talk for hours on end about work, family, hair (she loves a good product), fashion, fighting weight gain, and, of course, men and relationships. She brought us together in small groups or big gatherings. Sometimes, just whoever could make it found themselves enveloped in a love-inspired, uplifting, judgement-free, enlightening circle of women whose struggles, triumphs, hopes, fears, laughs, and tears would mirror their own: yesterday, today, or tomorrow. In my eyes, she coined the phrase "between us girls" because that's what it was. She, perhaps unwittingly, taught us the value of shared experience and the need to relate, release, and yes, rejoice. She was off-screen Oprah, Maya Angelou, Gloria Steinem, and Dr. Ruth Westheimer all in one - in red lipstick. I have never seen her without it. So, it's appropriate that a big red lipstick kiss graces the cover of this book where Marqueeta has done what she has all her life - unselfishly give other women a space to share with the rest of us what we see in our own mirrors: Ageless Glamour Girls™. So read, relate, release, and rejoice in a compilation of stories that will help you write or re-write your own.

Pat Battle, News Anchor/Journalist

Preface

"Just keep on living..." My late mother, the inspiration for Ageless Glamour Girls™, used to love saying this. I first heard it in my mid-twenties, but it didn't click until later in life when I began navigating this aging journey. And among many of our mothers back then, there was very little, if any, talk with their daughters about growing older, and all that comes with it. And the M-word? What the heck is that?

This void inspired me to want to share information and engage with other women on the same journey. My first foray into gathering and celebrating women came years ago when I set out to form the online group, Between Us Girls, and I secured the domain name, betweenusgirls.com. After my job began taking over my life, I somehow lost the domain before I got started in earnest, and when I checked it again, it was a porn site. Oh well...

Several years later, and still on a mission to become a vehicle to help women manage aging, I created Ageless Glamour Girls™, targeting women 50+. (I cover the origin of the name in my chapter.) My vision was, and still is today, to provide a platform in which women of a certain age can "gather" together and share information on various topics, including caregiving, finances, second acts, menopause, plastic surgery, dementia, sexual health, grief, incontinence, and everything else from finding love to finding the best mascara that stands up to hot flashes. Our goal is to inform, inspire, empower, motivate, and entertain through the voices of various experts and women sharing their personal stories.

We love uplifting and celebrating older women through various platforms, including social media posts on Instagram, TikTok, Facebook – the AGG website, and a private FB group: The Ageless Café, the Ageless Glamour Girls™ Podcast; and now an anthology: "Ageless Glamour Girls™: Reflections on Aging." I am THRILLED the women in this book chose to share their stories with me and the world. Get ready to be inspired, amazed, informed, and entertained! A huge thank you and shout out to my phenomenal co-authors! I love you, Ladies! #blessingsgalore

CHAPTER 1

Marqueeta Curtis-Haynes:
The Birth of Ageless Glamour Girls™

Age is just a number. Life and aging are the greatest gifts that we could possibly ever have. – Cicely Tyson

The Ageless Chatfest Journey

I've always been on a path to bringing women together for a chatfest, to keep us in the know. The vision for Ageless Glamour Girls™ – planted long ago, is partly fueled by my upbringing, my television news career of sharing information, and a need to connect with and celebrate women of a certain age. Long before Ageless Glamour Girls™ came on the scene, I created the domain betweenusgirls.com in the late eighties, and years later, I birthed Ageless Glamour Girls™.

A Firstborn Daughter's Dilemma

It began as a term of endearment: *Glamour Girl*. I don't recall my exact age when my late mother first greeted me this way, but I believe I was between 6 and 10 years old. After a while, it stuck.

I am Millard and Audrey Curtis's first-born daughter and middle child after my brother. Being the first girl brought lots of added pressure then and even into adulthood. My mother, who once graced a magazine cover, was determined to steer me toward becoming a lovely, upstanding young lady, pretty much created in her (Mom's) own image. That was the thing for many mothers of that generation. Years later, my sister told me that Mom was living her life vicariously through mine. It was a huge *Ah-Ha* moment for me. Everything became so much clearer.

My mother was born and raised in Dekalb, Mississippi, in the late twenties, a period marked by racial segregation. She was a beautiful lady, the kind who demanded and commanded respect. She was also very kind and extremely resourceful. Of course, family always came first. Mom was excited to have two daughters; she was very protective of us. However, she wasn't comfortable discussing the birds and the bees. She gave us directives on hitting the books and staying "presentable." When we were kids, Mom once told me and my sister, who is 4 years younger that even if we were going outside just to take out the trash, we should "comb our hair." She also once said, "Always wear clean underwear, even if they have holes in them. If you're in an accident, at least your underwear will be clean."

After high school, Mom attended business school and later became an accomplished computer programmer, while Dad, a Veteran who served in the U.S. Navy, later became a postal worker. She and Dad were always on a mission for their children to excel. But Mom took it a step further and wanted her daughters to live a "Charmed" life. Did you know that Sears Department Store used to have a charm school? During my early teenage years, I, along with my sister and my childhood best friend Sherry, attended classes every Saturday morning. The school was designed to teach young women etiquette, poise, and social skills. Later, in my early twenties, Mom gave me a book I still have, *The Allure Book - Be Irresistible in 21 Days*. She tried.

Longing to be a Mother

I don't have any biological children. I've always dreamed of having a daughter, and now often wonder what kind of mother I would have been. Would I have raised her as my mother raised me? What kind of relationship would we have had when she entered those challenging teenage years? My mother and I battled, until I got into my mid-20s, when we became Besties.

Not having my own children, after wanting them so badly for so long, has left a feeling of unrequited love that I've longed to share. I was 43 when I started dating my husband, and on one of our early dates, he asked me why I didn't have children or had ever gotten married. I told him there's never been an ideal situation for that to happen. I then told him I was working with a sperm donor clinic in California, with plans to get pregnant and become a single mom. He replied, "Hold on. I might want to help you with your plans." My husband and I tried, right after we wed. I was 44 at the time. But nothing. We then tried artificial insemination, but that produced nothing, except causing me to grow fibroids. I thought about adopting but didn't explore that further because

I was still trying to get through my grief of not being able to get pregnant.

But thankfully, God blessed me with phenomenal children, from others. I have two stepchildren, Amber and Charles; a nephew, Millard James; a niece, Maya Lynn; and the newest star of the family: a great-niece, Kennedi Audrey whom I adore, and who is also my Goddaughter. I thank God for all of them, every single day. And yes, I'm THAT Auntie – a *Fly Ageless Auntie* who will stop at nothing to protect my youngins' and smother them with love, and of course - gifts.

Hot Flashes and a Spare Tire

I grew up in East St. Louis, Illinois. As a teen, I remember seeing women gaining weight, especially in their midsections. I told myself I would not "let myself go" after getting married and as I grew older. As Mom used to say, "Just keep on living…" I didn't really "get it" until my early 50s when I started my menopause journey. It was ugly. I remember being in a department store's dressing room and was shocked at what I saw in the mirror: a spare tire sitting around my waistline! Then there was the apology to my husband because I had become so moody. The brain fog began, then the hot flashes – OK, *power surges,* which were out of control! While on a job interview once, I broke out into a major flash and alluded to the Florida heat as the culprit. Thankfully, the flood didn't stop that show, and I got the job! My husband occasionally pointed out the sweat on my face, saying, "Baby, you're sweating." No kidding, Sherlock. He knew exactly what was happening because I had explained it more than once.

Eventually, I started hormone replacement therapy and watched happily as the flashes began to subside and the waistline began to shrink. But a new gynecologist took me off the therapy immediately when he saw on my new patient intake form that my mother and other close family members had breast cancer. *Everything menopause* came back with a vengeance for several years. There was no "aging gracefully" in sight! And by the way, the flashes, which had stopped three or four years ago, recently made a roaring comeback! The brain fog occasionally rears its ugly head, though it's typically no match for my beloved cold brew coffee.

Planting the Seeds

Like many women of my generation, there was no discussion about menopause from our mothers or other older female family members. While "becoming," I struggled to find information on what was happening to me. I had many questions, including: what is this? How long does it last? Why am I gaining so much weight? What can be done to help alleviate brain fog? How can I fight menopause symptoms? Is it too late to start doing Kegel exercises? Is hormone replacement therapy safe? And most importantly, what mascara brands stay put during our natural, (not so) private, downpours. I knew I had to do something when my hot flashes began to ruin an otherwise great makeup job that I had done myself. I remember thinking there needs to be a group where women can get together to discuss these things. Surely, I wasn't alone in my despair.

All of this, along with my upbringing, inspired the creation of *Ageless Glamour Girls*™. We celebrate women of a certain age (50+) while helping them navigate the aging or *ageless*, or "ageless aging" journey, which can be tricky and challenging at times but also emboldening, transformative, and enlightening. AGG is a place to exchange ideas, share experiences, and provide nuggets of information and inspiration. AGG helps empower women via social media posts, shared articles, and information. The Ageless Glamour Girls™ Podcast discusses various topics, including building a new life after losing a mate, the job search, second acts, ageism, age discrimination, caregiving, finances, menopause, and other health topics including incontinence, dementia, finding a new love later in life, living your best life with or without a mate, getting your groove back in the bedroom, and so much more.

Stay Connected

As we know, this aging business can be challenging, making it even more crucial for us older women to be a part of a like-minded village. We often face social isolation, especially if widowed or have limited social networks. This obviously could mean fewer opportunities for us to connect with others.

We also might face a multitude of physical health problems, such as mobility issues, chronic illnesses, and cognitive decline, which can limit our ability to engage in social activities and maintain relationships. As we know, these health issues can lead to a sense of loneliness and dependency. As if that is not enough, other issues, including losing a spouse, family members, friends, along with economic insecurity, lack of access to technology, changing family structures resulting in you living far from your adult children or relatives, and ageism, can all lead to loneliness. While aging can be a hot mess, it helps to have a village.

Find Your Village, or Two, or Three

Find your community, and this could mean either online or in person. Engage, engage, engage! Tap into community support, i.e., local community centers, senior centers, and support groups that provide opportunities for us older women to socialize, learn, and engage. Of course, retirement communities can provide connections, along with co-housing arrangements. I read an interesting article recently about intergenerational programs that unite older adults and younger generations, such as mentorship programs or shared living arrangements, to combat social isolation.

And have you thought about volunteering or taking technology classes? There are initiatives out there that teach older women how to use technology, which can help you stay connected with family and friends through the digital world. The goal is to *stay connected*. Engagement is key. I like to think that the Ageless Glamour Girls™ community plays a role in helping women stay connected while navigating their journeys. We're passionate about helping women thrive.

Becoming

It's not too late, and you're not too old. Seriously. One of the beautiful things about aging is that you're much more inclined and motivated to do YOU. It's time to breathe – deeply and exhale. It's OK to say, "No." Explore. The world is our oyster! And whether you're team *#grayhairdontcare* or not, it's your choice. 'Not ready to publicly acknowledge your age? It's your choice. A little nip and tuck here and there? It's your choice.

Continue to move that body and that mind regularly. Surround yourself with those who keep you grounded, feed your soul, and bring you joy. Lead with love. Live with gratitude. Make time for YOU. And again, continue to engage with others, whether in person, over the phone, or by going "old-school" and mailing a written note or card. Take the time to listen to their thoughts, concerns, and stories. Sometimes, all someone needs is a compassionate ear.

Ladies, we deserve all the splendid things this life has to offer. It's our time! Never stop dreaming, and always stay curious. Let's show them what we've got! This reminds me of when 60-year-old actress Michelle Yeo made history at the Oscars. She became the first Asian woman ever to snag an Academy Award for Best Actress. When accepting her award, she said, "Ladies, do not let anyone ever tell you that you are past your prime."

My Personal Journey

I know *I'm* not…I'm still evolving, and I know that you are, too. I love the person I'm becoming. I'm still a work in progress; I'll continue to evolve. Do I have regrets? Yes, of course! And that's OK. They're considered life lessons, so I learn from them and move on. I look forward to embracing my second, even third act. Yes, there is life after television news; it starts right here with Ageless Glamour Girls™. Some call it a movement; others call it a great engaged community. I call it *love* for Ageless Glamour Girls. It's way bigger than me.

You know what they say: oftentimes, people see something in you that you can't or refuse to see in yourself. They see your bigger vision before you do. That reminds me of something my late father once told me, "Baby, you're your own worst enemy. Stop being so hard on yourself." And as Cousin Nevida (Turner), an uber 96-year-old Ageless Glamour Girl, says, "What God has for you is for you."

Cheers to Ageless Glamour Girls!

Your glamour is showing, and we love it, and it's illuminating the world! Here's to Healthy Aging and Joyful Living, Luvvies! Reconnect soon! Xoxoxoxoxo

The older I get, the more I understand that it's okay to live a life that others do not understand. – Unknown

Dress Your age! | She's past her prime! | She looks good for her age! | Blah, blah, blah! And still, we rise…

Marqueeta Curtis-Haynes Bio

Wife. Bonus Mom. Auntie. Great Auntie. Podcaster. Podcast Producer. Content Producer. Writer/Producer. Senior Producer. Executive Producer. CEO. People Curator. Entrepreneur. Photographer. Serial Overthinker, and more. Dream job: Professional Potato Chip Tester.

Details, Details

Marqueeta is a multi-Emmy-award-winning broadcast news Writer/Producer, with a career spanning from the Midwest to the country's top market - New York City, where she worked at CBS News, Bloomberg LP, and BET News. Throughout her adventures, she's garnered several awards, including three Emmy Awards, two Emmy nominations, and several Telly Awards.

The Beginning

Growing up in East St, Louis, Illinois, Marqueeta kicked off her career in the Midwest after graduating from Illinois

State University. She snagged a part-time gig at KMOX-TV/CBS (now KMOV-TV) in St. Louis, thanks to a college internship there. At the same time, she freelanced as a Reporter for a local newspaper. After a few months, she became the Chief Editor, making history as the first woman and African American to hold the title.

Later, Marqueeta ventured to California, where she worked in telephone sales for the Los Angeles Times.

Returning to St. Louis and the airwaves, she took on a role as a DJ and News Director at a Country-Western radio station. But soon KMOX-TV called her back, offering her a job as a Writer/Producer. That's when her career took off. From there she joined the CBS's flagship station in New York City, WCBS-TV.

During her time at CBS, Marqueeta made substantial contributions, from WCBS-TV to *CBS This Morning*. She also played a pivotal role in the launch of BET Nightly News, a news show produced by Viacom/CBS, as Senior Producer-Editorial.

After tying the knot, Marqueeta moved to Miami. She wore many hats, from Coordinating Producer at Nightly Business Report on PBS to Freelance Writer/Producer for a media production company. She was also a Senior Writer/Director for a studio producing talk shows for Lifetime TV. Marqueeta served as a Senior Producer at Black News Channel (BNC), a groundbreaking start-up based in Tallahassee, Florida. During her tenure, she played a crucial role in building and launching *BNC Go*, the network's cutting-edge streaming platform. Marqueeta is now the Executive Producer of a Florida-based, non-biased television news show: Power & Politics, which launches in January.

Outside of her career, she's the Founder and CEO of Purple Tulip Media, LLC, which provides content for various clients. PTM's offspring include Marqueeta's love: Ageless Glamour Girls™ (AGG), a celebrated lifestyle brand. She hosts a podcast of the same name. Additionally, Marqueeta manages a connected AGG brand - *The Ageless Café*, a private, vibrant community on Facebook, that serves as the "Chat Room" for AGG members. She also owns an ecommerce business, Purple Luci, which features items from Rwanda.

Marqueeta is a member of Delta Sigma Theta Sorority, Inc., and serves as a Board Member with the Press Club of Southwest Florida, formerly known as the Naples Press Club. She cherishes her roles as a wife and stepmother, godmother, auntie, great auntie, good friend, and enjoys finding joy in the balance between her personal and professional pursuits.

CHAPTER 2

Sandi Badash:
Aging My Way

I've never thought I was OLD! I'm sure others who know my age probably think I am old. I guess I would too if I gave it any thought, but I simply do not dwell on my age.

I've found myself describing others as older, then I realize they're younger than me! This always gives me a good laugh! So far, I see age as just a number!

I have two children, who are in their 60s, which means they're hardly kids anymore! I realize many people lost their parents when they were young, which is sad for the children and their parents. I'm happy that I've lived long enough to see my daughter and son get older and see who they've become as they aged. I think they're both wonderful human beings! I hope they feel comfort in knowing I'm still very much alive! My only regret is that we all live so far from each other. One lives in Massachusetts, the other in California, and

I am in Southwest Florida. I crave warm weather, and they want to live where there are four seasons! Plus, I have asthma, so I do my best at sea level. We talk a lot, which isn't the same as being in the room together, but while actual visits aren't as often as I wish, it keeps us together.

I'm an artist and I am very fortunate because I feel being creative keeps me youthful and always allows me to view life and things with a fresh eye. Perhaps, I'm a little on the quirky side because of how differently I see things compared to most people. This makes my life interesting and certainly not boring!

I was a bodybuilder in my 40s and 50s, which has something to do with me feeling and looking younger than my years. Also, I don't dress like most women in their 80s. People are often surprised when I tell them my age. I stopped coloring my hair and it looks great gray! I feel more like myself. It amuses me that very young women are dyeing their hair white or gray, and they look beautiful!

Like most women, I enjoy shopping, but I love shopping at thrift and consignment shops. I find more unusual clothes there than what I see in most stores, that I can put together in ways I feel are more *me*. I also love the *hunt*; it's one of my favorite pastimes!

In my years, I've learned the value and difference between friends and acquaintances. I limit my friendships to people I really enjoy, rather than having a host of acquaintants. I'm an only child, and spending time alone has become even more of a pleasure than it was in earlier times when I *had* to have my friends around me.

I no longer pursue constant male companionship as I once did. Instead of believing that a man is essential to complete my life, I now find joy in spending time with me. I realized a while ago that a male companion wouldn't make my life more enjoyable. I haven't and do not want to compromise on the things that matter to me!

And now on to SEX! I think it would be nice to have great sex every now and then, but to put it mildly, I really don't think men, for the most part, know how to really pleasure women. I've always said, "Men should spend as much time learning how to make love as they spend trying to become successful at work or watching sports!" Sorry men, but you good ones are in the minority, and it's not just me saying this! To be frank, pleasuring myself has often been more satisfying!

Now, let's see if I can find any negatives about being my age. Well, for one, I only wear long-sleeved clothing. Years ago, my wardrobe consisted of bikinis and full days walking on the beach. I was in my 40s and 50s back then. Today, I don't own a single bathing suit! When I was working out for competitions, I was very proud of my body; I was in the best shape of my life. Back then, I enjoyed going to nude beaches. If I was anywhere near a nude beach, no question, I was going! Today, definitely NOT! I do, however, know how to dress to cover my flaws, which I do have.

I'm sad that I never had grandchildren. Occasionally, I think about it and wish that I had grandkids. Unfortunately, neither of my children wanted a family. However, both married people who already had children, and both became grandparents; and they enjoy their roles.

My mother lived to be 102 years old; she was always healthy. It wasn't until the last week before she died that her health began to fail. I didn't mention it earlier, but I battled stage three Lymphatic Cancer. I had no symptoms when I was first diagnosed. I refused chemotherapy because I didn't want my quality of life to be undermined by the side effects of the treatment, especially at my age and not knowing what my lifespan would be! Fortunately, my doctor enrolled me in a research program involving various medication infusions, and I was cancer-free within three months. Now two years later, I continue in remission.

Also, I've had Covid THREE times, and it felt worse than when I had cancer. One of the downsides of Covid – at least for me, is that it seems to have robbed me of my singing voice, and I typically love to sing. But thank goodness I can still whistle, a talent my father taught me before I could even talk!

Here's the more recent kicker that has made me more aware of aging… Earlier this year, I fell and cracked three ribs! I had to use a walker while I healed. And fortunately, after about three weeks, I hardly felt any aches. However, because I don't understand how I fell, I must admit I have some fear of falling again. I don't like that feeling! But I must get over that – especially since I plan to eventually get back on the dance floor.

Life has had some glitches along the way, but for the most part, my *older years* have been a healthy and interesting journey. Again, I don't dwell on getting older. I hope that goes for you, too!

And by the way, the one thing that would bring me immense joy is to see a woman President of the United States.

Sandi Badash Bio

Sandi Badash is an internationally known author, artist, and jewelry designer. She's constantly involved in the creative process in one art form or another.

Her paintings, much of which are based on Cubism, an influential art movement that emerged in the early 20th- century- notably pioneered by Pablo Picasso and Georges Braque, are captivating! Her, stunning "neck-art" will take your jewelry collection to the next level and beyond.

https://www.instagram.com/sandibadash/?hl=en

https://www.saatchiart.com/Sandibadash

CHAPTER 3

Melinda Rinzivillo: Finding My Joy

A few years ago, I found myself standing in the middle of a women's consignment shop asking myself, "What have you done with your life? Where has your life gone? Have you REALLY *lived* your life, or has life *lived* you? Have you truly lived a joyful life, or have you only lived your life in response to the hardships and challenges you've faced?" It was as if a bolt of lightning struck me over the head right in the middle of the shoe department and yelled, "PAY ATTENTION! Time is racing on!"

I have no idea where these thoughts came from or why they raced through my brain. . . I mean. . . I was shopping! But I KNEW with complete certainty, that it was a "wake-up call," and I KNEW I needed to pay attention! I promptly left the shop. Now, if you know anything about me at all, you know that I absolutely LOVE, LOVE, LOVE to shop! But obedience summoned me to leave the store and I immediately started walking and thinking about my life – my career, my successes, my failures, and many of the decisions I made along the way.

Now, I know this may sound crazy, but on this day, I realized that I had spent 43 years of my life teaching. . . 43 years! I know many people dedicate even more years to education, but on this day, 43 years sounded like a lifetime . . . and when you really think about it. . . it was!

Forty-three years as an elementary school teacher for grades second through sixth. I was the "gypsy" of the school. . . always the one asked to switch grade levels. I was a gifted teacher, always challenging my students to think "outside of the box." Then a gifted coordinator; after that, a college adjunct Professor of Education; and later, a gifted specialist for a large Florida school district. Years later, when technology began to sweep the system, I continued in education working in special education, specifically with autistic children. What a humbling and extremely challenging experience. It was like none other – and one I will cherish forever! Forty-three years. . . Interestingly, I had never really stopped to consider how many lives I touched, or the contributions I made to my students and their families. It was as if I put myself on "cruise control" and went on a long career journey.

However, on that "shopping day," I came to a FULL STOP! I mean, I really stopped and reflected on what I had accomplished. I recalled that I played school from the time I was about 5 or 6 years old. I would create and grade hundreds of self-made spelling tests. I practiced how to write "C's" on scraps of paper for "correct" work and 100's for perfect spelling tests.

I also thought about how motivated I was to become a teacher. I had to work two and three part-time jobs just to put myself through college. I worked at a senior citizen residential hotel by day, and folded underwear in the lingerie department of Caldor's by night; only stopping occasionally to pick up a Ring Ding Junior and a Coca Cola for a quick (and very unhealthy) snack along the way. I didn't drive during my freshman and sophomore years. I thought about the train rides and the long, hard trek up that steep hill to the campus, especially in winter, carrying a huge pile of books. And for the first time, I felt a sense of pride in my accomplishments! I was truly proud that I earned three degrees on my own, and that I had overcome steep hills, slippery slopes, rain, sleet, frigid temperatures, and a myriad of other commuter challenges to become a teacher.

I thought about my students, too. Although every day was not perfect, my students were happy and always challenged. I had given them lots of opportunities to express themselves and their creativity in their daily assignments and projects. We worked hard, and we had fun, too. My students were taught to work independently and as part of a team, and to be critical thinkers and problem solvers. They were held accountable for their work and behavior. They were excited to learn and achieve.

Even after 43 years, my story did not end there. Finally retired and newly divorced after 20 years of marriage, I was uncomfortably back on the single's scene and devastated. I was young enough to enjoy my life but felt as if all my joy had been sucked out of me. I felt depleted. I knew true joy, that feeling of excitement and exhilaration I felt as a child on Christmas morning, came from within – and I was EMPTY!

I knew I needed to heal and recreate myself. With my teaching career over, I needed something else to dedicate my life to. I knew I needed to work on myself, to regain my sense of purpose and my sense of self again. . . I knew with complete certainty that I needed to dig deep within my soul and find my way back to happiness. I knew I needed a change of scenery, too. So, I decided to move to Naples, Florida, where I shared a condo with my sister. There, I would heal my soul and find my joy again. . . new home, new adventures, new experiences, new people, new hope, and new life. I barely knew anyone in Naples, so this would be a true "leap of faith!" Nevertheless, off I went!

My condo was beautiful. It overlooked a gorgeous golf course and had many fine amenities. But I was alone – and still empty. No friends, no family, and I was in unfamiliar territory. I spent my days trying to nurture my soul. I listened to my favorite music, walked the pier and beautiful beaches, collected seashells, and read scripture and spiritual books. I attended drumming circles in the park and even signed up for belly dancing lessons. I ate far too much pasta and way too many chocolate chip cookies. And of course, I went shopping! I spent days seeking out the best consignment shops and cafes – places where I felt comfortable and safe.

In my search, I came across one very special consignment shop called, "Audrey's of Naples." I LOVED it! Audrey's was eclectic! All the rooms were beautifully articulated and filled with the most unique, curated, and fashionable designer clothing, handbags, and accessories. To me, it was the MECCA of shopping, and I was in heaven! Every corner of the shop was mesmerizing. . . The sparkle, the beaded and bedazzled vintage bags, and Gatsby dresses. There was clothing from the '20s, '30s, '40s, and beyond. . . gala dresses, resort wear, and contemporary designer pieces; each with a unique story to tell. There was "eye candy" everywhere you looked! The shop, the staff, the ambiance. . . it was a shopper's paradise filled with pure charm and luscious fashion possibilities. Yes, I had found a new joy! I somehow knew I wanted to be a part of this magical place. My sites were set on working there!

I found my way into Audrey's first as a loyal customer. Today, I volunteer my time there. The owner loves my enthusiasm for her shop. She was the first to observe my raw talent for relationship building and people skills. She took me under her wing, nurtured me, and encouraged my growth. She was the first to recognize that I had color memory abilities, which was news to me! She was the first to call what I do for women a "Fashion Ministry." The owners of Audrey's showed me there was life after teaching and life after divorce. They embraced my gifts and talents and welcomed me into their Audrey's family. Now, I volunteer my time as an Independent Image Consultant/Stylist, and I couldn't be happier. Being with "the girls" at Audrey's gives me a great sense of purpose in retirement. I feel loved, valued, and appreciated – and in turn, I try my best to spread that same love and joy to the customers I meet. There's also a great sense of community and connection at Audrey's that energizes me and keeps me young-spirited and happy. It's artsy, creative, and FUN! I truly love every minute that I'm there! I love being surrounded by unique and beautiful vintage jewelry and clothing. I love that the merchandise changes almost daily. I love the challenge of finding women just the right outfits, colors, and accessories that work for them. I especially love "nudging" the ladies out of their comfort zones and challenging them to experience new colors, styles, and designs. The owner truly believes this is a "Fashion Ministry" for me. . . and I believe it, too. I smile every day. I spread joy to others, and I empower and help women feel valued, cared for, and beautiful.

I've been so blessed. I've met so many interesting and diverse people throughout my life from all over the world and from all walks of life. From inner city populations to suburban communities in New York, to the beautiful resort city of Naples, Florida. Everyone is on their own journey and has a story to tell. All my co-workers, friends, and connections made along the way during my years as a teacher, a friend, a family member, and now at Audrey's, have been life-enhancing.

I encourage you to try to smile through your dark days. Laugh often. Love and love some more. Seek and find your joy, and when you do – LIVE YOUR JOY FULLY and completely, without reservation or regret.

Melinda Rinzivillo Bio

A.K.A "Sweet Pea"

Joy is an emotional response that results from one's sense of happiness, sense of well-being, sheer bliss, and great delight. Finding your joy and living a joy-filled life is a choice. It requires vulnerability and a commitment to find happiness, especially during your most challenging times. It *requires* you to speak and live *your* truth. Follow this author's journey as she reflects on her years of teaching, weathering the storm of divorce, and finding new joy in retirement.

Originally from Westchester County, New York, Melinda now resides in beautiful Naples, Florida with her sweet cat, Pumpkin. She fills her days with music, shopping, dancing, comedy clubs, great friends and family, and a deep spiritual life, giving her joy and meaning.

CHAPTER 4

Karen Herlands:
The Antidote to Aging is Belonging

They whispered to her you cannot withstand the storm.
She whispered back, I am the storm ~ origin unknown

Ageism is real and it's ugly. My advice to older women is not to listen to societal opinion spouting what a certain age should look like, act like, speak like, or dress like. Forget all that noise! Any woman worth her salt will age into a ripe old woman, cocksure of who she is and what works for her.

I prefer to think of myself as ripening. Sweet and juicy may not be words to define women of a certain age, but spiritually, yes, as the years roll on, I'm more aware of just who I am. While I may not look the same as I did when I was younger, I continue to become more in focus with the creative, spirited, independent woman I call ME.

And being an older woman does come with a bunch of benefits. No more shaving. No more menstruation and no more kids at home to consume your day. And just maybe, if you are lucky, you've retired from your lifelong career.

Getting up when you want to; and spending the day as you wish; starting with a cup of your sacred drink of choice is a special gift of time that sounds pretty good to me. Slowing down to do all the things you said you wanted to do when you didn't have the time may require some re-adjusting, redesigning, and reassembling. Throwing away a coat that no longer fits may leave you feeling raw and chilly. Stay the course, be present, keep breathing, and soon you will learn to enter the room with more confidence than you could have ever imagined. I know this because it happened to me.

Moving on

I'm going to tell you a secret that changed my life. I'm (finally) doing all that I can to put myself first. And my advice to you is that you do the same. I can hear your heart beating because yes, it does take practice.

For me, it began to happen out of necessity.

The initial pivot happened in the supermarket when I stood frozen realizing that I no longer needed milk or anything else for that matter because the last kid had just left home. I started to cry and left empty-handed. I went to the Asian market instead, which is where I like to shop. In that very moment, I literally felt myself turn from externally always giving and feeling exhausted to internally listening to my own needs. It was an organic step that changed my life.

The second shift took place after we sold our house. It wasn't a huge home, but it always needed something, mostly my time and effort. I never realized how much brain time I spent taking "care" of the house until it was gone. It really freed up a lot of airtime in my head. It was in these empty spaces that the soul-work began to take shape. Swirling in a tunnel of noise, confusion, silence, and deafening doubts, I decided to run away. Well, I didn't actually run away; I booked a spiritual adventure. Destination: Southeast Asia. I visited family and friends, toured ruins, and temples, took cooking classes, boat trips, and visited small, behind-the-scenes neighborhoods. All the while breathing in and out, spending my newfound time confronting the new woman looking back at me in the rearview mirror. When I returned, I thought to qualify as a retired human you had to BE something. A golfer, a pickleball player, a yoga instructor, or a volunteer who works selflessly to save the world, or even write the next best-selling novel. I chose none of the above.

I enrolled in a program and became certified in Chinese Medicine and Chinese massage. I loved every minute of being a student. I found that I was good at diagnosing and relieving pain using special herbal formulas and giving deep tissue massages called Tui Na. I offered free advice to everyone who asked for help. It felt good to be good at something. I made business cards, got insurance, and even created a company name and logo. I was going to start a small woman owned business. Well, at least that was the plan.

Remember that time when the entire world stood still?

In March of 2020 the world came to a screeching halt! The COVID-19 Pandemic shut down life as we knew it. People went into their homes and didn't come out...for a very long time. We suffered a frightening two and a half years in our homes. We suffered through hoarding household items, empty store shelves; no toilet paper; baby formula, and even ice cream were nowhere to be found! Restaurants closed, Malls were empty and so were the roads. No one traveled anywhere. Lots of canceled plans.

But life in lockdown wasn't all that bad. Kids came home again. In fact, one of ours stayed for months and that was an unexpected, good thing! Watching Netflix was fun! Eating popcorn, nuts and snacks became a regular thing. I didn't care if I didn't have plans. It was refreshing to just "be" and relax.

But it was lonely. I wanted more than ever to go to lunch with a friend or two and not be afraid to touch or hug or share a dessert. But then, there was this little fact that I had lost a lot of friends for various reasons and felt very alone. Mother Nature had been cruel to many families, taking millions of lives. The world had become small and isolating.

When we took off our masks, a new world revealed itself. Many things went back to normal. Broken connections began to reconnect. Isolated family members could reunite. The streets were busy. People went back to living but the casualties of the Pandemic left an unimaginable toll.

Encore Post Covid

For a woman, part of feeling alive is about female bonding. There is an extraordinary connection to our inner selves, which happens when we spend time with other women. What's a life without a group of girlfriends to share stories with? Well, I no longer felt connected. I had lost those bonds. In fact, I was never very good at seeking out other women. I'm not sure what kept me from having lots of friends, but at this stage of life, I needed to change that ASAP. I needed some girl time, and I needed it now!

A childhood friend of mine reached out to me and we started to have lunch dates once a month. When I confided to her that I didn't have any close friends, she said, "Well, we need to fix that!" She invited me to join a local women's social club called ENCORE. At the first meeting, I was lost. There were over 100 women, and I didn't know where to begin or why I was even there. But I made myself show up to every meeting. Slowly, I began to sign up for several specialty groups. I told myself to join in, have fun, and be present. Eventually, I became a chairperson and served on the board of directors.

Becoming a member of a social group gave me a social life. There were lots of things to do and lots of women to do those things with. We all came for the same reason– we were looking to make friends; and I did. I found loving, caring, funny, sincere connections that completely made my life feel full and alive again. And I know we all feel the same way.

My friends allow me the pleasure to unleash the absolute best, and favorite parts of me; the ME I hadn't seen in a while. And we laugh a lot! Who knew that I was so darn funny? They stimulate a part of me I knew was in there somewhere but didn't know how to access– until I walked into the room and showed up. Connections are sustenance.

My wish is for you to know what that feels like too. When the Big Panda asked, in James Norbury's children's book, "Which is more important, the journey or the destination?" The Little Dragon answered, "The company." I couldn't agree more. Embracing the warmth of good friends who travel with you to your destination is truly the essence of a life well lived. Someday, you will retell your juicy story in your old age– whenever that is!

Saddle up.

Be a friend.

Have some fun.

Now giddy up and go!

Tally ho!

Karen Herlands Bio

Karen is a retired videotape editor who spent decades editing award winning documentary programs and news stories for air at CBS in NYC.

A move to historic Simsbury, Connecticut with her husband, Ross, and two children, Liza and Jared (and two cats) was like moving to a new country. Life was different from the streets she left in NYC. Slowing down was an adjustment which proved to be an unexpected, most joyful, creative time.

Learning to play the dulcimer, fingerpicking her guitar, she joined a band and performed for several years. During this time, she was also writing for a local paper, started a card-making hobby, worked for an elementary school as a paraprofessional and created monthly art posters for the school hallways.

Karen also enjoys hosting weekly Buddhist meetings in her home and chanting with friends.

She is a certified Whole Health and Nutrition coach, certified Chinese Herbalist, and Tui Na massage therapist.

These days, she mostly enjoys the company of friends and playing guitar with her husband, Ross.

Instagram: @herlandshealth

CHAPTER 5

Ciriaca Yolanda Sabio:
Choosing Healthspan and not just Lifespan

I've coined myself "The Anti-Aging Disruptor" because between me and you, I really hate the whole "anti-aging" world. It is full of statements that engender feelings of withering away, undesirable, full of physical pain, and uncomfortableness. Yes, we may experience some of those things, but it can be from other things, not just aging. So, I am here to DISRUPT that thinking, so that it doesn't sink into our psyche and "govern" how we see ourselves. As the Anti-Aging Disruptor, I coach women to daily choose Healthspan and not just Lifespan.

When I type the word "healthspan" it comes up as an error; yet the dictionary definition is: "The part of a person's life during which they are generally in good health, free from the chronic diseases and disabilities of aging. The goal is to enhance and extend healthspan." There is *lifespan* and then there is *healthspan*.

AGELESS GLAMOUR GIRLS: REFLECTIONS ON AGING

In this chapter, I am talking about intentionally choosing healthspan and not just lifespan. That intention permeates my daily life, and I hope that after you read this chapter, you too will embrace the wonderful experience of aging.

Personally, I want to live a long time; don't we all? I'd say I would like to live at least into my 90s and dare I say 100s! I want to live those years in a way that I am independent; able to get up, sit down, go to the bathroom, dress myself, bathe myself, feed myself, and get in and out of the car on my own comfortably. I want to be able to perform all the activities of daily living and not have to depend on anyone else. I am a dancer, not professionally, but anyone who really knows me knows I love to dance to all kinds of music. If the spirit of the beat hits me just right, I will instinctively move my body, tap my feet, swing my hips, and dance like nobody's watching. And if they are, I say just let them watch. I recognize that movement is vital to healthspan and I want to always be able to move my body without feeling aches and pains with every move. Can you relate?

Choosing Healthspan and not just Lifespan

If I were to boil it down to one word, it would be – FREEDOM. Freedom to live an unencumbered life. Is that asking too much? If you focus on what the media says, what certain employers believe, and what your family and friends may say, the answer is yes, that's too much to ask. But collectively, I believe we can change that. And we can change that NOW!

Right now, I am in my early 70s, in relatively good health, and I consistently and intentionally workout. Do I have some of the aches and pains that can be associated with aging, heck yeah. But I am glad to say right now (because who knows what tomorrow may bring), I am living an unencumbered life based on being mindful regarding what I allow to enter my mind, the way I eat, the physical movement that I do, and the social life I keep.

Where did this penchant for healthspan and not just lifespan come from?

Without really knowing it, it started in my early 20s, and sometimes I can't believe that it still pulls at me every day in how I live my life. I have lived 24 years longer than my mother lived, and that fact doesn't escape me for a minute. It was more than 50 years ago during the Christmas season; I came home from college for winter break, looking forward to a festive time with family and friends, with lots of traditional Garifuna foods, when my whole life was turned upside down. My mom, who had just turned 48 a few weeks earlier, went to bed with a headache on Christmas Eve and never got up the next morning. Instead, she had a hemorrhagic stroke and died in a hospital bed two days after Christmas. The doctors told us that if she had lived, she would live her life in a vegetated state. To put it lightly, that thrust me into a whirlwind. It wasn't until many years later that I realized its true impact on my life.

That impact became real one day, a regular very stressful day at work, when I was jolted by the possibility that a similar incident could happen to me. I was a single parent working a very demanding job that required a lot of travel and tight deadlines. One afternoon on an assignment in another state from where I was living, I got a tremendous headache that immobilized my ability to finish my work for the day. Before I knew it, I was on a stretcher being taken to

Choosing Healthspan and not just Lifespan

the emergency ward of the local hospital. There, I was diagnosed with high blood pressure; it was sky-high, and I hadn't realized it. This was my wake-up call! High blood pressure is known as a "silent killer," it can be generational, is often brought on by stress, or a diet high in salt, and has been deemed a lifestyle disease.

Up to that point, I had been walking through life feeling like a wet wrung-out towel. I thought everyone felt that way, that it was normal. It was then that I understood that I was not immune to the "silent killer." It scared me, and made me ask myself the question: "Was my mom's fate going to be mine as well?" Though I ate clean (I actually was a vegan in my 20s, before it became the thing to do), I was knowledgeable about nutrition, so much so that I wrote my college thesis on it. But, still, it got to ME. From then on, I lived my life holding my breath, as if "waiting to exhale," as I approached 48, the age my mother died. Once I reached 48, I got serious about living my healthiest life yet. I felt blessed to reach an age she had not.

I set out to get my blood pressure under control and did so through stress management practices, which I continue to do today. Having had to shop in the "chubby" department as a child (do they even have them anymore? I sure hope not), I also had to find ways to maintain a healthy weight. I tried a myriad of diets, from the low-fat/no-fat phase, not realizing that the fat was being substituted with SUGAR, drinking shakes, and eating bars as meals. I even went to the point of having pellets put on each earlobe, existing on an extreme caloric deficit, I tried WW, keto...you name it, I tried it all. And they all worked – for a time, but none were sustainable, especially as I got older.

It wasn't until I was clear on my "WHY" that my mindset shifted. If high blood pressure is a lifestyle disease, I will change my lifestyle. Through introspection and mindfulness, I began to understand why I ate what I ate, and how my body reacted to different foods. As I said, I love to dance and found joy in movement that helped me stay energetic and flexible, to the point that I became a Zumba instructor. I found joy in inspiring others to move, move, move. All of this came together to open my eyes and became my personal transformation. I am now in my best health ever!

Choosing Healthspan and not just Lifespan

We all have a tribe; I call my tribe, Seasoned Sisters, and I've added Sassy Sexy to it. Because you know, we all have a sassy sexy to us. Now, I'm not talking about Playboy sexy. I'm talking about the essence that is in each of us, that we sometimes try to hide so we can fit into society's version of what we should be like, dress like, and act like at our age. I take a stand for my Seasoned Sister, helping her live an active and healthy life for the rest of her life, helping her choose Healthspan and not just Lifespan! My work is in honor of the many women, like my mom, who never got to be a Sassy Sexy Seasoned Sister!

But where does a Seasoned Sister start?

Everything, and I mean everything, starts from the inside before it can be manifested on the outside. To step outside of your comfort zone and let your sassy sexy show requires a love of yourself and a certainty that you are who you say you are. It encompasses a trust in yourself, that "you've got you!" And it is enveloped by an unconditional love that makes you feel safe. I describe it as a "knowing." Yes, knowing that you/we are not here by accident. We have a unique purpose, and we are innately guided by that knowing. It is that knowing that speaks to us not so much in words, but in intuition, in gesture, in spirit. It requires you to tune in daily to what brings you joy, makes you feel good about yourself, and makes you fall in love with yourself over and over again. Why? Because this will keep you in tune with your essence. So, that's where you start. Right now, start with the belief that your essence is unique, and you are enough.

That belief becomes your barometer for the external. The external is all the stuff you read and hear about in the media and social media. Eat this, don't eat that, wear this at this age, do these types of exercises, compare yourself to this person... it all becomes NOISE that only distracts you and interferes with you being able to tune in to your essence. The distraction causes a stressor in your mind and body that causes an internal imbalance, which then manifests into physical, emotional, or mental dis-ease.

Choosing healthspan and not just lifespan daily takes work. That work takes daily commitment because it's the little things, the habits we develop that become our lifestyle, hence our healthspan. Besides your mindset, there is your way of eating and the movement that you do intentionally/ purposefully, and consistently. What that looks like on you may look very different than it does on another Seasoned Sister. You will want to experiment with what aligns with you, what brings you joy, and defines the results that you desire. While experimenting, focus on showing love and grace to yourself.

Let's look at your way of eating/nutrition. Should you go plant-based or be a meat-loving carnivore? Is intermittent fasting the way to go? What about the whole gut-brain talk you hear a lot about these days? I know, it can be very confusing and there simply is not a one-thing fits all. What I can definitively say is that you cannot rely on eating the way you did when you were younger. You will need to examine and ask WHY do I eat that way? More than likely, it is because, well, you've always eaten that way, it makes you feel good, it makes you feel safe, it subconsciously reminds you of a time in the past that made you feel safe, loved. Hence, it's your automatic go-to. Because it is automatic, we don't give it much thought until we get a scare, like I did with high blood pressure. Or, you notice you don't have the energy you once had; you try a new workout and get winded quickly. You walk past a glass window, and glance at yourself and you don't like what you see or don't even recognize that person in the reflection. We all get the wake-up call in one way or another. It is what we do with that call that matters. Most women know how they want to feel and look, but many don't put in the work to get the results they say they want.

Nothing changes until it is changed. One of the changes I have found in my practice that Seasoned Sisters may want to explore is lowering the amount of carbs they eat on a regular basis, especially for women in the US who eat the regular American way. Women in other countries may eat carbs, but it is the way the carbs are prepared, what they are paired up, what time of day they are eaten, and how these women live their daily lives that can make a big difference in what carbs do in their body. Here in the US, we have super-sized everything, not in a healthy way, and we generally move less.

Carbs mainly provide short-term energy that we need to use sooner rather than later, so they are essential. Depending on the type of carb: complex or simple, if not used in the short-term, it is stored as fat. In women it gets stored, mostly in our mid-section, and that becomes a constant reminder. You may or may not get to have that svelte body or firmer abs you had in your younger years, but you can change the composition of your physical body and feel, look, and be healthier. Focusing on the way you eat is a key element. Are you willing to change the way you eat and if necessary cut down on the amount of carbs you eat? You don't have to eliminate them, because as a mentor of mine said, "Anything taken to extreme can become error." You will have to examine your way of eating and make some changes. How willing are you? On a scale of 1 to 10, how would you rate your willingness, your commitment to change?

The next area to explore is Movement. You may call it exercise; I call it Purposeful Movement. The movement of your body allows you to use some of the energy you consume. There are all types of movement: cardio, strength training, high intensity interval training (HIIT), yoga, tai chi, qi gong, dancing, walking, hiking, and sports like tennis, golf, swimming, skating… There are so many, and they each serve a purpose in helping you stay healthy and energetic. What do you like to do? What did you like to do but now think, "I'm too old to do that." I say, do that. If you haven't tried it in a while, try it out "for size".

Just the other day, I took my young grandsons ice-skating at the local rink and dared myself to put on skates and get on the ice. You see, as a child I loved to go ice skating every Sunday at the local public rink and the thought of those times filled me with curiosity. So, I laced up the rented skates, and went on the ice rink. Can I tell you, I wasn't out there too long, but I enjoyed the exhilarating feeling of just trying! It brought me joy and gave me a fond memory. So, however, you choose to move, I encourage you to let it bring you joy!

Remain curious, and find what lights you up, because if it doesn't, you won't stick with it long enough for it to make a difference in your health. Sis, we can all agree that we have fewer years ahead of us than behind us, so let's make them count. You deserve to live our healthiest, happiest life yet.

You deserve to look, feel, and be as healthy as you can be, it just takes some work. How willing are you to put in the work?

I know you can do it. Take one element at a time and focus on being consistently good vs occasionally perfect. It is not a race, but **You Only Live Once**.

Choose Healthspan and not just Lifespan!

Ciriaca Yolanda Sabio Bio

Ciriaca (Siri-ah-ka) Yolanda Sabio, WiseNFit2

Ciriaca Yolanda is a Certified Health Coach whose mission is to Redefine Aging for the Seasoned Sister by helping her see in the mirror the person she's always envisioned in her mind she would be and enable her to experience breakthroughs in health right NOW. She coaches women to choose Healthspan and not just Lifespan.

Ciriaca is a 70+ year young grandma of 2 young boys, who believes that NOW is the best stage of life. She is passionate about throwing out the outdated stereotypes of aging and truly Redefining Aging in our lives and society.

Ciriaca has three tenets: *Mindfulness, Purposeful Movement, and Way of Eating*, which are intertwined in all her coaching programs and speaking engagements.

You can catch Ciriaca in a Kaiser Permanente Life Experienced short video where she talks about how she stays young, https://fb.watch/bmivzAS7Sz/, as well as her website: https://wisenfit2.com.

In addition, Ciriaca Yolanda has also appeared in the following:

https://podcasts.apple.com/us/podcast/teatime-midlife-edition/id1505135706?i=1000571007552

https://podcasts.apple.com/us/podcast/ageless-glamour-girls-agg-podcast/id1615786955?i=1000554995654

https://youtu.be/1jDtbRAyzuY

https://www.linkedin.com/in/ciriaca-yolanda-s-wisenfit2/

CHAPTER 6

Lisa Bedian:
On Second and Third Acts: Pull Out Your *Transferable Skills* Toolbox

Callaway County, Missouri, in 1990, sitting at the intersection of Interstate 70 and State Highway 54, isn't the place I'd foresee reflecting on as a major crossroads of my career. I asked myself a question that I'd asked several times during my 45-plus years (and still going!) career. Later that morning, I was starting a new job in the Missouri State Capitol of Jefferson City as the Chief of Staff for then Missouri Lieutenant Governor (and future two-term Governor) Mel Carnahan.

Back to the question, the first part anyway, and if you're an Ageless Glamour Girl or aspiring to be one, you've probably asked yourself: "What am I doing here?"

Maybe you've even answered yourself like I did: "There's got to be someone better, more qualified, who should be sitting in that chair today and starting this new job." What was I thinking? I didn't go to the "right school," my family didn't have the "right pedigree," and I didn't build my career path in this direction. I was first approached about this job in a bar in Kirksville, Missouri, a small college town where I'd spent three great years at what was then Northeast Missouri State University. Not exactly profile material in *Politico* or a Political Science professor's curriculum vitae from an Ivy League university. Yet, I was potentially becoming one of the most politically powerful women in the state.

What paths did I take to get to that intersection and continue building my career for another three-plus decades?

Here's the deal. I took the "open road" to endless opportunities. The fuel I used to power me was in a toolbox of transferable skills. You can, too. Being open to possibilities is exciting and challenging. We never know where the road will lead. You can focus on doing well, constantly learning, being curious, leveraging your skills, and building more while other opportunities suddenly appear on your path.

Many career experts have joined the chorus: "No one will be working for the same company for their entire (or most of their) career." A friend told me a while ago that I nailed the concept of transferable skills before it was even a "thing." My nickname was *The Job Vagabond*. My career includes stops in sports, broadcasting, and breaking several glass ceilings. I've worked in broadcast television management, healthcare communications, the defense industry, and local and state government. I leveraged my transferable skills, focusing on the opportunities, being accountable, and always seeking to learn more. You can, too! Ageless Glamour Girl, you can take the best of what you know and what you'll learn and create your own transferable skills toolbox.

We all have transferable skills. Choose to keep filling that "toolbox" and look toward the next opportunity to use those transferable skills. You may be in a challenging work situation. No matter how difficult, you can still learn new skills, be a high-level performer, and make the most of it. I've got scars and stories you wouldn't believe. I also took those skills, became more marketable, and increased my salary! No one can ever take those skills from you. *You earned them!* You'll be surprised at the opportunities that will open for you. The choice is yours!

Even if you're still a student or a recent graduate, you have skills you may not recognize. As an Adjunct Professor for over 25 years, I challenge my students to consider this perspective. Have you completed your degree or job training? You have project management skills. I don't know anyone who's ever undergone training or a degree program where all the classes, prerequisites, scholarships, or loans fell miraculously into place. To get that credential, you had to figure out workarounds, plead your case, and get deadlines met or extended. Guess what– lots of others didn't.

Many universities lose as many as one out of every four students who start but do not complete their degrees. Salute yourself if you did– and recognize those skills, including time management, budgeting, setting priorities, and meeting deadlines, all factors in your successful completion.

You may have accumulated your transferable skills from the school of life. Recognize them, and package them… Again, no one can take those skills away from you. *You* earned them! Before others see your sparkle, your competitive advantage, *you must see it in yourself first.*

On Second and Third Acts: Pull Out Your Transferable Skills Toolbox

Early in my career, I was a sports reporter in college and was the first woman to cover the school's football team for the university newspaper. I did it because I love college football. I wasn't looking to break any glass ceilings. As a decent track athlete in high school, I was asked to join the men's track team when I went to college. My top event was the long jump, so I literally jumped at the opportunity. I hadn't planned it or made it a goal, and I didn't think anything about being the only woman on the team or that Title IX had just passed a couple of years before. I just saw something I wanted to do, and I did it.

That's where my toolbox started, and I didn't even recognize it, or the need for it. Following my curiosity, taking advantage of the opportunity, and *learning* became my guiding stars. Plus, I had to fine-tune my creative banter skills and keeping a straight face. After all, I was the only woman on a team of dozens of college guys. Believe me, some of them made it clear they didn't want me there. They grumbled when the opportunities came my way, and *I made the most of them.* Not my problem. When people try to stand in your way or diminish you, *don't own their problem!*

I was also blessed with amazing mentors and became a sponge for the knowledge they so generously shared. I learned the lesson (and blessing) of sharing my knowledge with others and doing what's right. I honor and respect their memory by trying to be a good mentor. Thomas Jefferson observed the quote, "A candle loses nothing when it lights another candle." What a bright, beautiful perspective!

You miss opportunities when *you* don't recognize your toolbox of transferable skills. You're giving away your power– and your possibilities. I've made that mistake a couple of times in my career. Thankfully, Ageless Glamour Girls were there for me and helped me escape that place. Look around, you'll find them. Once you've broken through, you'll be ready to help others break through their walls, too. We lift each other up, we recognize our healthy and growing transferable skills toolbox, and most importantly, we're not going to give away our glory!

One of the most valuable traits you can have is being a lifelong learner. Curiosity, adaptability, and accountability will serve you well. Exploring new opportunities can result

On Second and Third Acts: Pull Out Your Transferable Skills Toolbox

in being off the mark sometimes. Mistakes and/or failures can happen, but I think the only time you truly fail is when you don't learn anything from the experience.

When I was younger, my dream job was to be a Color Analyst for a National Hockey League team. I ended up covering the NHL as a reporter, producer, and talk show host for 16 years. My professional career includes highlights like handling communications for the first successful use of a heart defibrillator in the world, covering sports events like the NBA Draft, World Series, NCAA Basketball Tournament, producing NFL game broadcasts, and many more. I've been part of a successful team that led to business development in St. Peters, Missouri, and 10-thousand new jobs. While in TV management, working with many nonprofit groups on events and awareness and generating thousands of volunteer hours worth millions of dollars for the community allowed me to use my skills while developing others. I also had to cover the tragic death of my former boss, then Missouri Governor Mel Carnahan, when his plane crashed during a campaign tour in 2000. I'll never forget working in health care after the 9/11 terrorist attacks. The common denominator is the value you bring with that transferable skills toolbox. By the way, one of my former interns, Chris Kerber, has been the voice of the NHL's St. Louis Blues for more than 22 years. I'm so proud of him and all he's accomplished! He's living his dream.

A former boss of mine shared a great observation with me, and I share this often with students, interns, and people I've mentored. "There are jobs that exist today that didn't exist five years ago, and there are jobs that exist today that won't exist five years from now." Think about this. Those transferable skills in your toolbox can set you up for jobs that don't exist today. How can you plan for those opportunities when you don't even know what they may be?

Keep learning and growing and be open to the possibilities. You may be approached about jobs from very surprising sources. I've been contacted or "courted" with some interesting opportunities. Imagine answering the phone, and the familiar voice on the other end says, "I want to tell you about a job, and before you say no, hear me out about why you'd be perfect." Pull that "straight face" skill out of the toolbox!

On Second and Third Acts: Pull Out Your Transferable Skills Toolbox

Now—back to where we started on this Ageless Glamour Girl's journey on a mid-Missouri highway in 1990. I was on my way back home after the first few days on the new job at the State Capitol. With a couple of hours on the highway in front of me, I had time to consider the question I asked myself on the way down to Jefferson City: "What am I doing here? There's got to be someone better than me." My answer: "I'm exactly where I'm supposed to be– *I am the right person for this job!"*

Here's to a chorus of Ageless Glamour Girls shouting that answer! And don't forget to bring your toolbox!

Lisa Bedian Bio

Lisa Bedian is a passionate storyteller, strategic thinker, leader, and lifelong learner. Working in state and local government for more than 20 years, she's won 25 communications and broadcasting awards. An adjunct professor of sports marketing, she broke glass ceilings in sports broadcasting early in her career. She's bilingual in Armenian and an active community volunteer.

https: www.linkedin.com/in/lisa-bedian-039b143

CHAPTER 7

Dionne Jones:
The Unicorn:
A Journey of Grace, Healing, and Rarity

I don't take lightly the gift of grace. As I reflect on the journey it took for me to become the Unicorn, I am grateful for the Divine. Born in the winter of 1970 to young hope-filled parents, I would have suspected that life would be grand. Rainbows and Unicorn filled even! A life of love, and stability.

My parents were in their early twenties when they married and began their journey into parenthood. Dad enlisted in the US Army and was stationed overseas for my first year of life. I don't recollect the details but through oral history and photos, I can see and feel that I was welcomed into this world. Welcomed with a promise of love and security. The first photo of my birth was that of my mom holding me in front of our family home in the Outwaite projects.

We hear projects and our minds travel to despair and violence, but in 1970, my mother assured me it was quite the opposite. A safe community that looked out for each other. A community where I was wrapped in love. Wrapped in security. My dad returned stateside, and the adventure began! An adventure that would be filled with happy memories and many firsts. Our first stop was Texas.

Texas was the most stable time of my childhood. The fondest memories of childhood come from this time in my life. My 5th birthday party, the feelings of happiness, the carefree life! Surrounded by my family and friends. I still vividly see and feel that experience as it was what we imagine childhood to be. The gift of a kitchen set with a bold blue table and white chairs still brings a smile to my face. There would be many Tea Parties thrown at that table. The pink-paisley pillow would also live vividly in my mind for years.

I was madly in love with the ginormous pink paisley body pillow. It was my safe place. My imaginary land of rainbows and unicorns was created on that pillow. A safe place that I would have to retreat to in my mind to save my very soul in the next decade of my life. In the Fall of 1975, my pillow would be lost to the birth of my younger brother, but I digress. It was a good thing my dad, the Lab Technician, had watched a film on labor and delivery 24 hours prior to the destruction of the pink and paisley pillow. I remember being awakened by my godparents standing by my bed because I would be staying with them for a few days. As I slowly became aware of the total picture, it dawned on me that my brother could not wait. Mom was in labor at home and my dad was delivering my baby brother on my pillow in the living room.

As I walked out with my godparents the EMS team arrived and transported my parents to the hospital. The memories of the heat, red ants and my blue round plastic pool will remain with me, as those were the happy days of my childhood. It was the grace of this foundation of security and happiness that I clung to survive physically, mentally, and spiritually when life took a sharp turn.

Military life entailed frequent relocation. Our next stop was the Presidio in California when I was 7. There were happy memories of speeding down the hill and spinning out in my Green Machine. I loved my school and friends. Life began to shift as I turned 8. I was blessed with a little sister during this time, and all seemed perfect. I had the beach down the hill, the fastest Green Machine on the block, my own room, and not a care in the world. My dad would sit me down and tell me we were moving to Ohio to be closer to our family. Not fully understanding the implications, I cheerfully looked forward to being able to spend time with both sets of grandparents, uncles, aunts, and cousins!

We packed up and in that very instant my world was shattered. My mom, my cartoon buddy, my hair slayer, the best hug giver, was not coming with us to Ohio. She stayed in California. I couldn't wrap my mind around why mommy wasn't coming. That day I learned what divorce meant. We moved back to where I was born but without my mom.

We settled in my paternal grandparents' 2-family home. I didn't adjust well because I was missing my mother terribly. Feelings of hurt and confusion permeated my spirit and I cried myself to sleep the first month. It was in the tail-end of 4th grade. I slowly began to withdraw and stick to myself which made me an easy target for bullying. I hated Ohio! I hated school and I hated my mom for leaving me.

My dad was doing the best he could to raise 3 children ages 2, 5, and 8. My paternal uncle and grandparents were a great source of support. My paternal grandfather, a factory worker, always made it a point to spend time with me. Sober or inebriated, but he was my safe space and just a few steps away if I needed a great chat. My maternal grandparents were instrumental in getting us to church every Sabbath and making sure I received a Christian education from the SDA Academy around the corner from their home. Most of our weekends would be spent at their home and some evenings after school. Things seemed to be stabilizing.

When I turned 10, whatever foundation of normalcy I thought existed was ripped away. My dad lost his footing while drowning in his own grief of divorce. He began to be gone for long periods of time, leaving me to fend for my younger siblings. Little did my 10-year-old know what the next 6 years would bring and how they would alter my trajectory. Years of chaos, child endangerment and abandonment would tear through my family and leave years of anger, hurt, confusion, fear and instability for me and my younger siblings.

Healing

Dad struggled to keep the facade of stability going as he got deeper and deeper into his drug use. He went from working full-time and going to school to being out in the streets or passed out at home. All I knew was that my siblings and I needed to be taken care of and it fell on me. I didn't know how to be a provider in my preteens, but I loved my siblings enough to at least try. My Paternal Grandmother had her own struggles of dealing with several of her 6 remaining children either in the streets or substance abusers, so she did not want to face the reality that another one of her children was on drugs.

Growing up fast would leave a hole in my heart for several decades. Home was not a space for me and my siblings, but it was the hand we were dealt. God sent a neighborhood family that would provide a temporary safe space for my spirit that kept my mind safe, and I will be forever grateful for this saving grace.

In The Color Purple, Sophia stated, "A girl child ain't safe in a family of men," especially men who were chemically dependent. I don't remember who molested me first, my father or my maternal uncle? All I knew was that home was not safe and now my maternal grandparent's home was no longer safe. I told no one for fear that my siblings would be taken out of the house, and we would be separated. The imaginary land created in my mind when I was 5 years old would be my mental escape during the incidents of sexual abuse. It protected my mind from shattering coupled with the one true safe space I had in the home down the street. This abuse arrested a healthy adolescent development and created many trust issues. My childhood and adolescent years were accelerated and stifled concurrently. My growth was accelerated because I was in survival mode, but I was not able to have a full experience of innocence, childhood, or adolescence.

It all came to a head when I was 16 years old. I felt a positive and safe energy around me as my father crept into my bed. An energy that would give me the physical strength to fight him off the top of me for the last time. I will always remember seeing the glow and being grateful for that Divine source that closed that door in my life, as that was the last time my father attempted to sexually abuse me. My Maternal Uncle moved out of state and that allowed that abuse to stop. Years later, my father got clean, finished school and was back on track to the father I knew and loved before the abuse, but the road to forgiveness would be long. We made huge strides when he came to me and asked for forgiveness. I have given it to God and have forgiven him but am still working on extending grace to my father. It did not happen overnight, and it is not 100% but at the age of 52, I know holding on to the pain is not and was not an option.

Our family was torn apart due to being abandoned and abused at home. My heart breaks for my younger brother because I can not save him. He has a hole in his heart that he is not ready to fix, and it is painful to watch himself destruct. Not having stability, love and safety as a child wreaks havoc on your self-esteem, your self-confidence, and your ability to dream. I look at my siblings and want to just wave a magic wand and restore their spirits and fix the hurt. But I know it is a healing journey they must first take alone and then as a family. The work is ongoing, and I am grateful to have my mom and sister back in my life.

Unfortunately, my Maternal Uncle is still depended on drugs. He did ask for forgiveness some years ago. For my peace and growth during my healing journey, I keep my distance, as he is not ready to heal. My mom and I are healing, discovering each other and I am grateful for that. Grace has been extended to me and I know that I too have the responsibility of extending that very grace!

This journey of healing has opened my eyes to the patterns of abuse that occurred on both my Maternal and Paternal side of the family. The very pattern that nearly shattered my soul, I had not been the first to experience in my lineage. As I look at the lives impacted by sexual abuse in my family and how it stunted growth and the trajectory of dreams, I knew that I would not repeat this cycle! I would heal myself. My children would be loved, protected, and allowed to grow and dream of a brighter future. The curse would stop here!

It is a journey of peaks and valleys. Grateful for more peaks at this point in my life. There are days that a trigger will present to remind me that this is not an overnight process and has led me to phenomenal natural modalities of healing.

Rarity

Fitness launched my healing journey. Working out allowed me to get my physical body together, and to channel my anger and hurt into my workouts. Beginning the healing journey was extremely difficult. It was easy to stay mad! Hide behind the mask! It had become easy to go through the motion. Be numb. A battle versus the evil that happened to me and the happiness I sought on the other side of healing was a daunting task. Self-doubt, low self-esteem and little to no self-worth were no place for any vibrant women to reside. The start of my healing journey opened my eyes, heart, and mind to what was possible for my future.

Therapy would take what I had begun with fitness and allow me to regain the inner essence of happiness that had been covered in decades of pain. I didn't realize I was suffering from Post Traumatic Stress Disorder (PTSD). The mask even had me believing I could skate by and continue to suppress the hurt I experienced daily. Therapy gave me back the strong sense of security I felt before the abuse. Learning that I was and am enough was empowering. Learning not to blame myself for what ill adults did to me as a child was the part of my journey that accelerated my healing and growth. Forgiving myself for blaming myself propelled me into starting my business to help other women heal. Forgiving my father and maternal uncle released me from the self-imposed prison I had placed myself in for decades. Therapy would leave me with a sense that I was more than a survivor of sexual abuse, I was a rarity. I was a Unicorn.

I lost my connection to faith as I questioned the Divine for letting me experience sexual abuse during my childhood. As I began to heal, I reconnected to my Spiritual center and was able to see that this pain didn't happen to me to break me, but instead it happened to create the advocate that was needed to be a voice for other women still needing to begin their healing journey from childhood sexual abuse. I don't have the answers for what this advocacy will evolve into, but

I know for certain that the Divine chose me for such a time as this. I know now that it was Grace from the Divine that protected and sparked the courage to begin and continue my healing process.

Lastly, my trusted village was and continues to be a part of my healing process. Amid living in numbness and fear as an adolescent, the Divine sent a family of Earth Angels whose home and love would protect my mind, soul, and sanity. The love they gave to this wounded little girl provided a glimmer of hope for a brighter future.

Today I look back on my journey of grace, healing, and rarity, grateful for the life lessons, the Earth Angels, the discovery of happiness, love and what my life at 52 has become. I am excited for my future, my advocacy work, and the impact I now know this Unicorn was born to make!

Dionne Jones Bio

Dionne is a Gerontologist, Licensed Social Worker, Author, Certified Personal Trainer, and Wellness Coach. She is the founder and owner of Age with Vibrancy LLC in Cleveland, Ohio. Age with Vibrancy LLC is a holistic wellness company with a mission to provide curated fitness and wellness programs for women aged 40 and older who feel stuck and need help starting their wellness journey. Age with Vibrancy LLC uses holistic, mind, and body philosophies to assist clients in reaching their health and fitness goals across their lifespan.

She is a fervent supporter of her community. As such, she is the current president of the National Coalition of 100 Black Women, Inc. Greater Cleveland Chapter; she also serves as the co-chair of the National health committee. She is a proud member of Alpha Kappa Alpha Sorority, Inc. She still gushes at the mention of her husband of 26 years and is the proud mother of 2 grown sons.

@agewithvibrancy and https://linktr.ee/agewithvibrancy

CHAPTER 8

Lynn Venhaus:
You Are Not Alone: Dealing with Grief and Loss

For about a year after my oldest son died, every morning, in that transition between sleeping and waking, I would imagine it had all been a dream, and he was still alive. Then reality would quickly set in – no, Tim was gone. Forever.

After Dec. 9, 2018, it would take every ounce of my energy to get up and face the day. Staying in bed and avoiding the world was the preferred alternative.

A budding filmmaker and dedicated teacher, Tim beat to a different drum. With a rebel yell and a pilgrim's soul, he made his mark during his brief time on earth. He was mostly at home in front of or behind a camera. He loved to make people laugh.

My very humorous, creative, kind, considerate, big-hearted, beautiful boy brought so much joy to so many. Sure, he could be impatient and sarcastic and struggled to control his temper, but he was fiercely loyal to friends and family and good to his mama. He could read the temperature of the room to sense what was needed.

Oh, to hear him laugh one more time… I miss him telling me, "Chill, Mom! It will be OK." He calmed me down when I got stressed, anxious, or overwhelmed.

The loss of my son has been life-altering, as if my arm were cut off. Sure, I can live without a body part, but I will never be the same. I am resigned to that feeling. What else can hurt to that magnitude? I can't imagine any pain greater.

Death is final – the end of hope and dreams, no longer physically existing. There are no more texts, calls, coming or going, hugs, celebrating special moments large and small, and sharing news.

What I miss the most is no longer seeing the world through his eyes, learning things from him – how he would point out an indie movie, a rising star comedian, a new song, or a local neighborhood joint or his random observations –

his unique way of telling a story that you'd never forget. There's so much about him that I long to have more of.

Tim was such a bright light in our lives. He had special relationships with so many, and they all have stories to tell, many about his kindness, especially to his students. The "Tim-isms" will always make us smile. People told me how much he influenced their tastes, how he was a thought leader, and what an impact he made.

On the back of his tombstone, we had a line inscribed from the song "For Good" from the Broadway musical "Wicked," which says, "Because I knew you, I have been changed for good."

Nearly five years later, the loss seems more pronounced. The reality that there are no more memories to be made is an ever-growing ache. Everything is in the past, in the rearview mirror. The hole in our hearts has grown, not gotten smaller. Three major deaths in the family within four years have taken a toll, and just like that, nothing will ever be the same again.

Now, every holiday and special occasion has empty chairs. My younger brother, Matt Zipfel, a dynamic junior high science teacher and coach forced to retire due to a terminal illness (Multiple System Atrophy), died nine months after Tim. My beloved uncle, a widower and retired mailman, Charlie Zierrath, died in July 2022 after his 90th birthday. Their absence is deeply felt.

My other brother, Mike Zipfel, has been missing since last seen on Jan. 6, 2005, but that sad song has its own very long chapter.

My son, Timothy Robert Venhaus, passed away on Dec. 9, 2018, at home in his sleep. He turned 34 a week earlier and was a thriving graduate student in the MFA Screenwriting program at DePaul University. I had never seen him happier, from his time as a finalist that March to the official acceptance, to figuring out where to live in Chicago (with a friend in Logan Square), and then being on fire telling me about his classes, eager to chart his future.

He was finally pursuing the path we felt was his destiny. It had been a long, non-linear journey. Still, filmmaking was something he had been passionate about since his childhood. Making movies with friends and families, being mentored by Dan Cross at Southwestern Illinois College, receiving an associate degree in film, and then earning a bachelor's degree in cinema production from Southern Illinois University Carbondale were all catalysts to him finally pursuing his dream. While at SIUC, he interned at "Sesame Street."

Oh, the places he went! What an adventurous soul! From 2005 to 2017, he taught at Nature's Classroom, an outdoor environmental education program at 13 sites in New England, where he worked for spring and fall periods. He taught filmmaking to youths for two seasons at Summer Fenn, a program connected to a prestigious private school in Concord, Mass.

Hole in Heart, Empty Spaces

He was looking forward to returning to school on Jan. 5, 2019. He was hired by a performing arts school in Naperville, Illinois, to teach filmmaking at an after-school program on Fridays early in the new year.

While home on holiday break, he worked a seasonal job at a nearby restaurant, making money for his travels and school expenses.

That Saturday, he had worked a grueling double shift, walked through the back door, and announced he was exhausted, so he was going straight to his bedroom. We exchanged "good nights" and "love you's," I shared a couple of top-vote-getters in the St. Louis Film Critics Association's annual awards voting, as I had just arrived home from a nominations tally session. Watching all the "For Your Consideration" awards contender movies had been an exciting tradition during our Decembers for 10 years. I found out later that he had written in his journal on Dec. 7, "Having fun watching movies with mom."

He was supposed to work the Sunday brunch shift, and we surmised later that he couldn't sleep (texted two pals at 3 a.m., they told me). He took something he shouldn't have, which ended his promising life.

Before they took him away in a body bag, a city medical examiner asked if it might have been suicide. We were emphatic in our "NO!" The ME told his father and I that it would be six weeks to two months until a death certificate could be issued. That's how backed up they were. When it was released, the cause of death was "Acute accidental fentanyl intoxication."

He was one of 1,608 overdose deaths in Missouri in 2018, which was the #1 leading cause of death among adults aged 18 to 44. He was now a statistic, and we became members of a club no parent wanted to join.

As we are all painfully aware, loss is a fact of life, and everyone processes grief differently. It is not something you get over. Instead, it is something you learn to live with – and it's a struggle. It is an unfathomable depth of sorrow unlike anything else. One you can't know, understand, or explain until it happens to you.

Of course, your routine is forever altered, and that ache will always be in your heart. Little things blindside you – triggers will set off waterworks at the unlikeliest times and places: the grocery store, a song on the radio, a photograph.

One of the reasons I wanted to share my journey is that, as Gloria Steinem says, "The healing is in the telling." Another is to help others realize *you are not crazy or alone.*

My mind replays finding his lifeless body that Sunday morning, still in bed. I had been busy finishing the SLFCA work before our annual gathering. As secretary, it was my responsibility to send everyone the nomination tallies, and then we would break any ties before releasing our announcement. It was always a festive, fun day with my colleagues. (Awards are a big deal in film critics groups).

I realized that he may not have left for his morning shift. His car was in the driveway. Yet, the house was eerily quiet. I was unsure if he called off, because he complained of a sore throat Friday, or if he'd just overslept. No coffee was made, and no sign of him getting ready in the bathroom. Something, or someone, was nudging me to check on him. I had this feeling that something wasn't right. As I was about to leave for the SLFCA meeting, I knocked on his door. "Tim, did you call off?" No sound. I called out to him again. No answer, just stillness. Then, I slowly opened the door, hoping to find him groggily waking up in a panic because he had missed work or grumbling at me for disturbing his slumber. At least, that's what I hoped.

Instead, I approached, feeling that it was bad. I saw an ashen face frozen in time, a surprised expression, a foam 'cone' at the right corner of his mouth, and some dried blood coming out of his nose. Oh, no! Ooh, No! I knew.

The first person I called was Kent Tentschert, my Webster-Kirkwood Times colleague and treasurer of our film critics group. We were the tag team that got everything ready for the meeting. I had to explain that I wasn't coming, for the first time since 2008, so he'd have to take over prep.

I don't even remember what I said to my son, Charlie, who had to arrange a flight home from NYC, or to his dad, Bob, who came right over. Then I called 911, "No, he can't be resuscitated," I told them. I estimated death occurred some hours ago. Somehow, my reporter skills kicked in.

Although his bedroom was down the hall from mine, I heard Tim snoring very loudly around 3 a.m. when I woke up for a bathroom visit. If only I had known that was a sign of fentanyl intoxication suppressing the respiratory system, which was later explained to me by a police officer. Perhaps we could have gotten Narcan to administer… but I know we can't 'shoulda, woulda, coulda.' But still…

Then, two policemen rang my doorbell. "Do you think it is drugs?" I asked them. "Oh, ma'am, it could be any number of things," one said. "I am being realistic. He has been sober for two years. I don't know if he was taking anything, but he has in the past." (I'm from a family adversely affected by generations of alcoholism and substance abuse). "Oh, ma'am, we see this every day. It's an epidemic," one said. Everything after that was a blur because I was in shock.

Word spread quickly. People were so incredibly kind; all the messages, texts, visits, food deliveries, cards, letters, donations, memorials, and showing up for the visitation and funeral Mass were very comforting. I don't know how else we could have gotten through that week and the days and months ahead. We will forever be grateful for the outpouring of affection.

Life became "Before" and "After."

We had to learn how to be normal again. It felt like operating on autopilot.

That fall of 2018 had been a triumphant first trimester in film school for Tim. While on break, he enthusiastically talked about his professors, what he learned, how they responded to his ideas and work, and what he would take the next trimester.

He was planning to attend a friend's wedding in Florida on New Year's Eve and visit a friend in Maine around the holidays. He had places to go and things to do.

That first year without him, I was reminded of the Courtney Love album, "Live Through This," produced after her husband Kurt Cobain died. When a day was tough, I'd say to myself: "Live through this." That emptiness can crush you.

People would comment about my strength, but I felt a mess. I'd say variations on "Well, I have another son that needs me, and the electric bill must be paid." Joy and interest were missing for things once special, and those "firsts" were just awful to endure.

My family watched helplessly as my younger brother, Matt, declined from a rare neurological disease with no known cure. It robbed an otherwise fit athletic coach and teacher of movement, digestion, sleep, continuing his job, caring for his three beloved pet Siberian huskies, and staying in his home. He left this world on Aug. 31, 2019, on his 59th birthday. I found his lifeless body when bringing over his birthday dinner.

Also declining was my dear, sweet Uncle Charlie, a father figure since I was 7. He was in failing health for a few years and was in hospice during his final days at a nursing home. To witness a transition is a profound experience. He was a highly regarded good man, always there for us, and now he is at peace.

In July 2001, I watched my 70-year-old mother die from lung cancer, surrounded by family, as we removed life support at Barnes Jewish Hospital. We encouraged her to let go. She had been in ICU for a month, now unresponsive, vitals astonishingly low, but waited for my brother, Mike, to arrive from Dallas. She briefly opened her eyes, smiled, and then took her last breath. It was peaceful. She was so loved. At her visitation, one person said, "She made you feel better by being around her." Yes, she did.

I thought that was the worst thing to ever happen to me. Life can swiftly turn, as we all know. Waiting for the other shoe to drop is a terrible feeling.

My faith gives me hope that in the afterlife, I will see my son, two brothers, uncle, mother, grandparents, and close friends that I've lost too soon to cancer. We don't know what heaven is like, but if it is as we are led to imagine, love never dies. That keeps me going, even as grief seems to consume me some days.

Death is simply a fact of life. No one gets out of here alive. I get it, and you get it, too. Still, this does not make it any easier to let go of your loved one. Whether it's expected or not, accepting death is difficult. Grief will always be the large elephant in the room, manifesting itself in many ways, ready to bring your day or night to a halt. And that is the 'new normal.'

There is no right or wrong way to deal with grief – it's personal. Every experience is different. This is mine, and I don't present myself as an expert. After the worst thing happened, I'm learning as I go how to just get through another day.

How you feel is valid. Don't ever feel there is a timetable. Be kind to yourself. Listen. Learn. Love.

Had we not had support when facing these big challenges, I don't know how we could have endured. I recommend leaning on others as the best advice I can give. Do not shut people out. Take people up on their offers to help. Peace and comfort are elusive, but reaching out and being there is such a gift from another person. It's soothing, heart-tugging, and means so very much.

Be mindful that many well-meaning people don't know what to say. Just know people care, but everyone handles tragedies in different ways. After someone I knew experienced a loss, such as a parent or grandparent, I would offer my condolences, and sometimes, they would respond with some version of "Well, it's nothing like yours, losing a child." I would reply with (paraphrasing): "Loss is loss. It doesn't matter how old they were, the circumstances, or how long you knew them. We shouldn't quantify grief."

When trying to maintain composure, unfortunately, triggers are everywhere and can easily thwart your best intentions. A reminder of one of my oldest son's favorite things can easily reduce me to tears. You know certain times will be hard – holidays, special occasions, milestones, but it's the random pop-ups that stop us in our tracks.

It's important to me to keep Tim's memory alive, to make sure he's never forgotten. It's very strange and awkward to talk about him in the past tense. I cling to the treasured memories his friends share, which makes my heart happy.

Writing for newspapers since I was a teenager, work had always been a vocation, a major part of my identity, something I threw myself into with great drive and stamina. Yet, being Tim and Charlie's mom was the absolute best – the most rewarding and fulfilling experience of my life. These precious humans entered the world in 1984 and 1988.

During their adult years, I cherished every moment I spent with them, as Charlie moved to Brooklyn in 2011 and Tim was away often – working or attending school. I am very grateful he came home for that year before he went to grad school.

While he will remain an eternal, vibrant presence, it hurts that I won't see him flourish in the career he was so passionate about – and closing out his life was tough. But 'What if?' is a fruitless exercise.

Ah, human frailties. There is such a stigma to drug-related deaths. Addiction is a chronic disease, not a moral failing. Tim struggled and tried very hard, but it won. It's hard enough to be in mourning, let alone stress that his life had worth, value.

With the encouragement of his DePaul professors, we produced his last screenplay, a dark comedy short, "Dad Eat Dog," which was accepted into the 2020 St. Louis Filmmakers Showcase.

A committee from DePaul University's School of Cinematic Arts paid tribute through an award, The Tim Venhaus MFA Thesis Feature Screenplay Award, given at their annual Premiere Film Festival on June 7, 2019.

One of his classmates wrote to me: "Tim was a real gift to our class." A professor told me: "He was a great addition to our program."

On the year anniversary of his burial, his mentor, Dan Cross, arranged a "Tim Venhaus Retrospective" at his community college. He described him as his most productive student. We laughed and cried in equal measure.

Then, the global pandemic hit. The anguish of social isolation was profound. We got through the public health emergency, but for those of us in mourning, it felt like a double whammy.

What's the takeaway? Human connections are crucial to health, physical and mental. Having solo pity parties won't move us forward. Seek counseling if you feel stuck. There's no shame in getting the help you need.

Think your feelings out loud.

All we can do is our best. I confront inertia, and concentrating can be difficult. However, distraction is easy. I remind myself of the serenity prayer: I can only work on what I can control and accept that I can't control everything.

We all share something – we will carry our lost family members and friends with us forever, and their memories will be a blessing.

Finding purpose is a way to carry on, and that's why I will continue to spread awareness of the fentanyl national health crisis in America. So many lives have been ruined.

Wrestling with his demons, Tim made a terrible mistake. Fentanyl is involved in more deaths of Americans under 50 than any cause of death, including heart disease, cancer, homicide, suicide, and other accidents. It is responsible for about 200 deaths a day.

Naloxone is a medication that can reverse an overdose of fentanyl and other opioids, such as heroin, morphine, and oxycodone. In March 2023, the FDA approved over-the-counter sale of naloxone. You can carry it and keep it at home.

I plan on joining other mothers in efforts to ensure that our sons and daughters did not die in vain. They mattered. #WearetheMoms. We can turn pain into action. Tim will be the shadow ever looming with me for all the days of my life…

To my fellow mourners, I leave you with these wise words from Maya Angelou: "My wish for you is that you continue. Continue to be who and how you are, to astonish a mean world with your acts of kindness. Continue to allow humor to lighten the burden of your tender heart."

Lynn Venhaus Bio

Lynn (Zipfel) Venhaus has had a continuous byline in St. Louis metro region publications since 1978. She writes features and news for Belleville News-Democrat and contributes to St. Louis magazine and other publications. She is a Rotten Tomatoes-approved film critic, currently reviews films for Webster-Kirkwood Times and KTRS Radio, covers entertainment for PopLifeSTL.com, and co-hosts podcast PopLifeSTL.com... Presents.

She is a member of the Critics Choice Association, the Alliance of Women Film Journalists, and the St. Louis Film Critics Association. She is a founding member of the St. Louis Theater Circle.

She is retired from teaching journalism/media as an Adjunct College Instructor.

She currently lives in St. Louis and grew up in Belleville, Ill. She is the mother of two sons, Charlie Venhaus, who lives in Brooklyn, NY, and the late Tim Venhaus (1984-2018).

Facebook: https://www.facebook.com/lynn.venhaus/

LinkedIn: linkedin.com/in/lynn-venhaus-48284616

Twitter/X: @VenhausLynn

Instagram: lynn.venhaus

Podcast: PopLifeSTL Presents (formerly Reel Times Trio)

Website: www.poplifestl.com

CHAPTER 9

Cheryl Collier:
My Grand Journey

Back in 2008, my son and daughter-in-law told me they were going to have a baby, my first grandchild! I remember thinking and saying aloud, "I'm not ready to be a grandmother, I'm too young to be a grandmother." I'm sure that's not the reaction they were hoping to get.

Honestly, I wasn't trying to ruin their joy and make their news about me. I guess, I was apprehensive because I had some preconceived notions about what it meant to be a grandmother. To me, it meant I was getting old and people would view me as being old. I was 49 years old, and I thought people, like friends, coworkers, and other colleagues, would think I was old. Clearly, at the time, I worried too much about what other people thought of me.

I didn't have any experience to draw from with my own grandparents. My parents were older when I came along. I was born the day after my father's 40th birthday, and my mom turned 40 about six months later. My dad's mother died before I was born, and I met his father about two times. My mom's father died when she was a child, and I visited her mother only a few times when I was a child. So, I didn't really know them.

When my husband and I had our three children, my parents and my husband's parents were in their sixties and retired or close to retirement. After retiring, my parents moved to Atlanta and his parents moved to Los Angeles, both very far from where we lived in New York City.

A few years later, when my husband and I moved our family to Atlanta, we lived with my parents for a few months. Our children saw their grandparents every day; and I saw how my parents behaved as grandparents. They were firm, but definitely more indulgent with their grandchildren than when I was a child. My dad would take my youngest, his little three-year-old granddaughter, to the store and buy her whatever she wanted.

Fortunately, we were able to send our children to visit my husband's parents in Los Angeles during summer breaks from school. They made great memories and formed loving relationships with their grandparents. They had lots of free time to spend with my kids. I learned a lot about the role of being a grand from them.

Still, when it was my turn, I was not ready. I was working in my career as a journalist. I had more than a decade to go before retirement. I had some gray hair, for sure, but I didn't feel old. And what would my new grandson call me when he started talking? Would he call me Grandma? I thought that would surely make me seem old. My daughter-in-law suggested that I should choose my own Grand name. Should it be Granny? Or Nana? Maybe Gigi or GeeGee, or how about Grand Diva? I think I saw that name somewhere on social media. After thinking about it for some time, I decided that my new name would be Grammy, which is kind of funny because I can't hold a tune. So, I'm pretty sure I will never receive a Grammy Award in this lifetime.

When my daughter-in-law gave birth to a beautiful baby boy, I was overjoyed. He was adorable! He looked just like his dad. It was wonderful having a baby in the family, a little bundle to hold and feed and just stare at in awe. It was like having another baby of my own, but without all the morning sickness and queasiness, and the whole painful labor and delivery deal. He was the only child in the family for five years, and we spoiled him a little.

It was really fascinating to learn about the things that had changed since my children's birth in the 1980s. I learned that doctors in 2009 told new parents their babies didn't need to drink water because water was already in breast milk and baby formula. New parents were told not to put cereal in formula in the bottle. Doctors also advised new parents not to put babies to sleep on their stomachs and not to put pillows and blankets in the baby's crib because that could lead to suffocation and sudden infant death syndrome or SIDS. Oh, and the walkers with wheels that my kids used to scoot around the house and learn how to walk were no longer considered safe. There were so many new and interesting gadgets for new moms and babies, like bottle-warmers, automated breast pumps, and boppy pillows for snuggling babies.

Then in 2013, my older daughter got married. The next year she gave birth to a baby boy, and he was such a little sweetheart! Then about a year later she had twin boys! Identical twins, who were born in late May under the Gemini sign. We had no experience with twins in our family, so it was fascinating to watch them interact with each other, their exact duplicate. When they were toddlers, they would sometimes switch personalities, which made it even harder to tell them apart. It took me about seven years to finally, definitively be able to tell them apart. It was crazy!

In case you haven't been keeping count, by 2015 we had four grandsons. Months after the twins were born, my husband and I bought a house big enough for all of us. We all decided to live together and share the expenses in a multi-generational household. Two grandparents, a grown son with his wife and son, a grown daughter with her three young sons, minus her ex-husband, and another grown daughter. Yes, that's right, there were ten of us living in one house. Maybe we were crazy, but it worked for us. When the parents in our group were at work or went on a trip, we, the grandparents, were there to help. We were the built-in babysitters. We have large communal areas like the kitchen, the dining room, and the family room. We also have our own rooms for privacy, a space to get away from everybody when we need it.

Then in 2017, my son and his wife welcomed their second child, another bouncing baby boy!

That's five grandchildren… all boys with all the energy in the world. I guess they were typical boys, all rough and tumble. They played pretend games, they would play-fight, and they are loud! It's fascinating to listen to them playing with each other or fighting against each other on video games on their cell phones. They accuse each other of cheating all the time. When they shout commands and suggestions to each other, they use great vocabulary and of course, there is the usual name-calling and insults. Their favorite insults are about somebody's hairline or big forehead; just like my kids did when they were little.

You know how adults sometimes wonder where kids pick up certain behavior, phrases, or attitudes? Well, I don't have to wonder anymore, and here's why. Whenever I ask one of my twin grandsons a question, his first response was usually,

"I have no idea." It seemed like a random and oddly specific answer. So, I started to wonder where he got that phrase. Then one day, my daughter asked me a question, and I very easily and casually replied, "I have no idea." But was I mimicking him, or did he get it from me? Who knows? But it goes to show that kids are always watching and listening to the adults around them. It also shows that we can learn from them too.

Sometimes I look at us, like when all eleven of us go out to dinner at a restaurant, and I realize how extremely fortunate, some would say blessed, we are. What started as a random meeting between me and my husband on a New York City bus, turned into something pretty special. But the story about that random meeting back in 1976 is for another time.

Our separate lives evolved into a family of eleven individuals who share unique talents, lots of laughter, some major challenges, and always love for each other. I realize that even if I could, I wouldn't change a thing about my life. I am a grown woman with a satisfying career, a wife, a mother, a friend, and a grandmother. My Grand journey has been amazing and it's still going strong.

I've learned to not care what other people think about me or what I do. My mantra is "qué será, será," which means, whatever will be, will be. Who knows, maybe one day my fervent wish for a granddaughter, a little girl, will come true.

Cheryl Collier Bio

Cheryl Collier is a storyteller, writer, producer, and media specialist. She is passionate about using the power of words to captivate, motivate, and inspire. After earning a degree in Broadcast Journalism at New York University, Cheryl began her career in news radio in NYC, then moved into television news and never looked back. Her journalism career took her to Atlanta, where she worked for decades as a Writer, Producer and Segment Producer. Cheryl is also a wife, a mother of three grown children and a grandmother to five smart, curious, and energetic boys. When she's not working, Cheryl enjoys reading romance novels, sewing, and traveling.

https://www.linkedin.com/in/cherylcollier

CHAPTER 10

Maria Gonzalez:
Life Lessons and Observations of a Mother

Life throws you all kinds of curves when you are not ready. Think about that for a minute. We would be bored out of our minds if everything in our lives were preplanned, no drama, everything just perfect. Well, buckle up, buttercup, and enjoy the ride; there is no such thing as perfection. We strive to achieve perfection. To paraphrase legendary singer Prince, "Dearly beloved, we are gathered here to celebrate this thing called life."

My name is Maria Gonzalez, and this is a snapshot of my life. When I was around 10, my sister and I took our family's TV apart. Yes, apart. It was a Saturday morning, and we were supposed to be doing chores. Instead, we were playing, and I was acting out a scene in front of our television. After a few minutes, I had a bright idea… what would it look like if I were on TV. Armed with a screwdriver and my imagination, my partner in crime and I dismantled the television and created programming. Little did I know that would be the start of a most fabulous journey.

My first published piece of literary art appeared in the local newspaper that summer. I won first place in a poetry contest. As I progressed in my education, I loved to write historical vignettes rather than boring history reports. I am thankful that my eighth-grade teacher allowed me to express my creativity to my classmates, eager to play the parts in my historical, hysterical one-act plays.

In high school, I was in the choir, on the fencing team (the boys' team), and in the drama club. I was also a speaker for the DECA club, an organization designed to help high schoolers excel as future business leaders and entrepreneurs. It included public speaking contests. I recall one event for the Knights of Pythias when I was so nervous standing at the podium. My upper half was calm and collected, but my legs and knees were shaking. Ever the performer, I used my nervousness with comedy as my speech was about getting over stage fright. The audience and judges thought it was hilarious; I recall them laughing when I slapped my leg and commanded it to stop shaking. Oh, yes, I won the event.

By the time I got to college, I had turned down a scholarship to The Juilliard School. I could have been the next Kathleen Battle if only in my mind. I attended college in New Jersey, where I studied Psychology, a noble profession. The problem was it was not creative. I auditioned for the radio and television department; once accepted, I found my tribe. I loved every aspect of this field: writing, producing, and directing. Senior year was hectic. I worked my first paying job in the industry at NBC New York, answering phones and doing polling research. From there, I scored an internship in the Broadcast Standards Compliance and Practices department, allowing me to write the show synopsis for *The TV Guide* and preview the weekly show rehearsals for SNL (Saturday Night Live).

About a month before graduation, I attended a media hiring event at Howard University in Washington, DC. This event was open to everyone; however, only Howard's students were allowed to be interviewed. I spent the day walking around the exhibit hall, absorbing information about the different companies in attendance. I zeroed in on two companies, and I waited until the end of the day and approached their booths. At one of them, I did a one-minute elevator pitch for an ABC executive, and at the end of my pitch, I asked for his business card. This gentleman was so impressed by my bold approach, not only did he give me the card, when I finally called him, I got the job - cameraperson for ABC Network in New York City.

During my stint at ABC, I worked on a variety of programs, including 20/20, Good Morning America, All My Children, Ryan's Hope, and The City, as well as ABC Sports and the local ABC News TV station, Eyewitness News. I met notable news personalities including Barbara Walters, and Joan Lunden. I was fortunate to meet celebrities, entertainers, politicians, and global dignitaries like Gloria Estefan, Billy Crystal, Robin Williams, Senator Ted Kennedy, and even Panamanian military leader, Manuel Noriega - each name mentioned has a story for another day.

You never know where a chance meeting at a symposium on Cable can take you in life. I met a man who essentially changed my life because of a question I posed to the panel. He sought me out after the conference and offered me a job at a cable company in Jersey City, New Jersey. It was the chance of a lifetime to create something that did not exist. I jumped in with both feet! I had the opportunity to bring my visions to life. During this time, my team and I designed the studios. We built a remote studio truck, control room, editing room, sets, and created programming. I was enjoying my creative freedom. I did all of this in nine months. During this time, I was married with one toddler son. By the time I launched the two channels for the cable company, I had given birth to my second human creation, my youngest son. I have such unforgettable memories working with my production team at City 3. Some of my most notable memories involve being at the first WrestleMania event, where I met Wrestler Hulk Hogan; interviewing Mike Tyson; meeting a man with a unique voice, Vin Diesel; being kissed on the forehead by South African Leader Nelson Mandela, and having my pregnant belly rubbed by Mario Van Peebles.

After the birth of my second son, my life took another direction, and I taught a television production course at a local community college. I enjoyed teaching. I served as the Director of Media Production and Technology, working with students, community groups, and the like. It was an extension of my work with my former employer. Essex County College was a unique environment where I worked with students and attended events with politicians, educators, foreign dignitaries, and entertainers such as Whitney Houston, Raven Symone, and even African royalty.

Life has a way of propelling you, and whether it's forward, back, left, or right, there are always things to learn and new people to meet. After leaving academia, I went to work with another local cable company to be closer to home. Raising two young boys requires a lot of attention. Soon, I found myself needing a challenge and went to work briefly for CNN in New York, where I monitored live remote footage. During this time, I saw two major news events that deeply affected me: a live shooting in which the camera person died and the Flight 800 crash aftermath. It was around this time that I got a call from Roger Ailes; yes, along my journey, I met this man. We had an interesting relationship, yet another story for another day. He had just gotten the head honcho job at FOX News and offered me a job. When they were launching, I went to work for them, and they were using the slogan "fair and balanced." This was the beginning of Fox's entry into the news game and the first time I experienced hitting the glass ceiling as a technical manager. I was the only woman on a team of 10, misogyny in its raw form. Early on in my career working in the news, I made a conscious choice to be apolitical and not to voice an opinion about politics.

Around this time, I was looking for more control over my career, and I began to select jobs based on creativity, education, and positivity. I became more involved in working on small and low-budget film and television projects. I found myself on the New York Launch team of BET, where I had the time of my life! I was cliff jumping and building something amazing and unique once again. We had about six weeks to build sets, create technical teams, and rehearse programs scheduled to air with live audiences. Some friendships forged in the long workdays are still going strong. Many notable entertainers came through the doors of the 106 & Park studio. There are the stories I usually share over a few cocktails, but I'll give you a bit of a teaser: Snoop Dog, Whitney Houston, Bobby Brown, and LL Cool J. "Ladies, he is a hugger and smells delicious." Those celebrities aside, it's heartwarming to see the newbies that I hired and nurtured in the early 2000s, still working in the industry today, along with the seasoned pros I worked with over the years come together, making one big family, each person unique and talented.

In the years since BET, I have been teaching Television Production at another local college, writing, and producing independent films and other video content under my brand, Little Black Dog Productions. Right before COVID came into our lives, I began to transition to my second act becoming a voice-over artist. I started this new chapter by lending my voice talents to a nonprofit organization that helps children. I loved reading to my sons when they were young, so using my storytelling skills to help a new generation enjoy learning and books was just a natural progression for the mom/educator in me.

Now that you know my back story... When I sat down a few months ago to write this chapter, I had a lot of beautiful words and testaments about getting to "the Middle Ages," which is where I am in my life right now. However, I concluded that I am nowhere near ready to slow down. As I see my friends and colleagues retiring, I'm just getting started with my second act.

What did I learn since I became a conscious adult? A technique I call "cliff jumping" was how I challenged myself, whether it was a career decision or something as simple as figuring out how to buy an expensive pair of designer shoes when on a shoestring budget.

The things that I learned in my life are pretty simple. You will laugh so hard that you will experience a release in your bladder. You will sneeze so hard you will have a release in your bladder. And if you get momentarily frightened or startled, guess what your bladder will release. So be prepared in every scenario of your life with a backup plan.

As I mentioned, I am a wife and mother to several humans and fur babies. I have two biological children, and I was blessed to help raise a third child. I love them all. They have three different personalities. The comic is the one that keeps you laughing until you cry. Also, there's the one I call the attorney, who loves to debate every situation, and the spitfire with a heart of gold. It can be challenging to navigate these personalities and give them what they need as a parent while they are young. As parents, I know many of you can relate. The baby phase is easy; you love and nurture. From toddler to adolescent, you give more love with nurturing, understanding, and setting boundaries. Now, we are crossing the border into the dreaded phase of raising children from teens to young adults. No book can help you. Each child is unique. What works with one doesn't work with the other. You may experience periods of elevated blood pressure, and your alcohol consumption may increase. You can go from an occasional social drinker to I need a drink daily. Around this age, your child may be trying to explore just how far those boundaries you have laid down can be pushed. Your teen will get their driver's permit around this time, and most parents have gone gray or started to lose patches of hair. With the license comes a sense of freedom, an escape from the watchful eye of parents and onto the most challenging of all, the young adult phase. When do you stop being a parent? NEVER! When do you stop caring and stressing? NEVER!

When are you considered obsolete? Almost immediately after they turn 21, but you are called back into the role immediately after the first big life mistake. Yes, you are the Fixer, especially if you are the Mom: Giver of advice, Fixer of boo-boos, and a personal banker with a 24-hour ATM. You might hate the person who broke your baby's heart for the first time and then accept that person back into your life when they make up or get married to said person. It's a symbiotic, psychotic relationship that makes you wonder if it's worth it. It is. It's the rollercoaster called life with children.

Raising children is like growing plants that talk back. Now, it's just me and the dog watching Hallmark movies and eating ice cream until I get a call or a text for the next emergency "dumpster fire" to extinguish.

Grandbabies are the best thing to happen to parents. They give you all the love, hugs, and kisses you could ask for and more. They are small and enjoyable. You hug them, kiss them, and buy them presents. Spoil them, let them eat cake for breakfast, and then they go home and drive their parents up a wall. Ah, the cycle of life continues.

I learned early on that in relationships of all kinds, whether it's business, friend, lover, boyfriend, or husband. There is no such thing as a 50/50 relationship. Who was the idiot who coined that phrase? There is always one person that does more. Relationships can be 60/40, 70/30, or even 90/10. Sometimes, this fluctuates due to circumstances. I always say, "You don't seek equality in relationships; it will never be a 50/50." If you understand this, you will survive and save yourself a ton of money in therapy costs. You also must know that you must listen to your inner voice. Expectations and reality are two opposites. You cannot change anyone. The only thing that you can change is your environment and yourself.

What makes me get up in the morning? Life! I'm happy to breathe freely, stretch, walk, and dance. I love to dance and could never fulfill my dreams of taking dance lessons as a child due to a lack of money. Then, as a young adult with a career, I was too busy raising children and working. It only took a knee replacement, an ad in a local newspaper, and a doctor telling me that I would never be able to wear heels or dance again to inspire me to prove him wrong and fulfill a lifelong dream. Today, I am a competitive Latin ballroom dancer who dances in heels. I am blessed to have an outstanding professional dance partner who deals with my quirky personality. Thank you, Juan Ramirez, and your lovely other half, Dasha Ramirez Gidaspova, for providing such a loving and nurturing environment that inspires me to train harder to achieve my dance goals.

A friend once said, "To live life right, you must look at each day through the eyes of a child." A new day is another chance to play, see friends, ride your bike, or eat a messy ice cream cone on a hot day and bite the bottom to see if you can eat it before you get brain freeze and a cold, sticky mess running down your face. Who has time to do these things? I'm so busy. It's crucial to your well-being to look up, look around, and truly experience life. Taking the time to nurture yourself is vital to your well-being and staying connected to your inner child.

Friends come, and then they go. I have experienced this at several points, and maybe you have, too. I'm talking about the transient people that come into your life. I feel they are sent to teach us lessons. They appear from nowhere to help us in a crisis. Sometimes, they are there for a reason, a period of time, and when they have completed their mission, they disappear like the angels they are!

Some things about me... I don't like to be lied to or used without my permission. I'm not a clone of my mother. I have always been unapologetically me. I'm not your average wife and mother. I don't bake cookies; I create those bad boys. I love to create through cooking, poetry, stories, pictures, and films. I am a creative person but don't ask me to draw anything. I know my limitations. Am I cocky and full of myself? No, I'm just comfortable in my skin. Growing up a military kid means you don't have the luxury of having the same classmates through grammar and high school. You are always the new kid. I adopted the philosophy that walking into a room full of people is an opportunity to meet and possibly make a new friend. This philosophy has helped me not only in school but also in life. My second rule of thought is not to take yourself too seriously. I'm the girl who gets all dressed up and trips over nothing.

I'm not hung up on education, economic status, expensive cars, or homes. Some of my most treasured memories involved exciting conversations over a well-cooked simple meal shared with real people, sharing what they had with someone they barely knew. It was humanity at its best. Money does not make the man or the woman.

Music has always played a big part in my life, so much so that I have songs that I refer to as my life soundtrack, the heartbeat of my existence. As I write this chapter, I realize my playlist is rather eclectic. My first song is Maria by Michael Jackson. That's no surprise, right! Then there's Tea & Sympathy by Janis Ian and Angela Bofill. Her music got me through the first tumultuous year of college, including the loss of my grandfather, my parents' separation, my first major breakup, and my devastating fencing knee injury. The works of Stevie Wonder and the movie soundtrack from "Somewhere in Time" evoke sweet memories of my wedding. During the darkest times of my life, Elton John's "I'm Still Standing" was my response to all the life drama swirling around me. As time progressed, the song that got me through family drama was "Survivor" by Destiny's Child.

One of the most surprising things I discovered at my college graduation party was that my dad, Eddie, could sing as he and two male friends belted out "Reasons" by Earth, Wind, and Fire. Music was and still is a driving force in my life narrative. My mother, Elizabeth, was a musician, and several family members, like Fred McFarlane Sr. and Fred McFarlane Jr. Junior, co-wrote "Show Me Love," performed by Robin S. I know you all are creating beautiful sounds in heaven. Thank you all for enriching my life with your gifts.

When I reflect on my life's journey, it feels like only a short amount of time. Then I look at my sons, who both have beards and mustaches, and at my spitfire with a heart of gold who is now married with two children. My children are all grown up with lives of their own. In the blink of an eye, life happened. My husband, Doug's, beard shows gray hair, and my hair is now dirty blond. We are still in good health and active. Our parents are gone. Time is moving forward at a quickened pace. Have I become a watcher? I used to refer to older people who read the obituaries daily to see who died as *watchers*, and now we have Facebook.

I think not! I'm not ready for a rocking chair, gray hair, or the traditional grandmother's house dress. I will be in a dance studio doing the mambo, traveling the world, making new friends, writing, or making a film, doing voice-overs for video game characters, and living life. Don't wait for someone else to get a clue to present you with a happy-ever-after. I'm out here making my happy ending. I hope you make yours.

Maria Gonzalez Bio

Maria's career spans over 35 years. She has worked for network, public, cable, and television channels and has been an independent film producer for several films and many video projects. She created and launched two local cable channels and worked on both the FOX NEWS Channel and BET Television launches in New York in a managerial capacity. Her unique skill bank includes management, staffing studio facilities, television programming, production, and budget management. She's also a producer, director, and screenwriter. Maria has taught broadcasting and TV production courses at two colleges and for community and church groups, and a tween summer camp. She produced *Coming Up Easy* and won the 2005 Best Feature Film at the Reel Women International Film Festival. Maria is an ACE Award-nominated producer and published author, who develops television and film projects for her company, Little Black Dog Productions.

Maria is enjoying the second act of her television career as a voice-over artist, narrating several books. She's also working to develop educational and animation projects.

https://www.facebook.com/profile.php?id=1600612095
https://www.instagram.com/mg2ari/
http://Linkedin.com/in/maria-gonzalez-49760310

CHAPTER 11

Marian R. Featherson: **Butterflies**

Born in the South, there were certain things that we were taught. One being... anytime you walk into a room, you speak. So, thanks for inviting me into your room. Hello, how are you? Really, how are you today? Honestly, how are you? I hope today is better than yesterday. I want to spend some time with you, let you know a few things about me while celebrating and acknowledging glamorous you.

My goal is to make you smile at least once today. I intend to get you up, going, and thinking. I want to let you know you are Beauty-Full. Okay, go ahead and get what you need. May I offer a few suggestions?

- Water
- Coffee & Bagel
- Tea & Crumpets
- Wine & Cheese

- Mimosa & Lox with Cream Cheese
- Orange Juice & Egg Cheese Biscuit
- Margarita & Chips with Salsa
- Sunflower Seeds
- Donuts anyone?
- Do not forget your sexy specs!

When I think of life and what we go through, butterflies come to mind. Butterflies quietly move about with no harm or threat. Some people may think that is likened to a woman, as if all we do is move or walk around looking pretty. They don't know that most women are moving about making things happen. Believe me, if you stop moving, so will many things around you. Think of a few things that you do, and if you change your routine or course, it throws everyone else off. Now *that* will get someone's attention. So, I encourage you to keep it moving, and look beautiful while doing it.

Butterflies are said to be among the most exquisite creatures in the world. Just like women, they catch the eye, come in all colors, and are just gorgeous. Like butterflies, women are mesmerizing to observers. Both go through life cycles and stages. Butterflies have four stages. As glamorous and ageless women, we must have *at least* nine stages or nine lives... to do all that we do. Just like a butterfly, we go through stages in life that make us who we are, resulting in one of nature's most elegant creatures.

My love for butterflies is because they are each different. In all my years, I have never seen an ugly butterfly. They are all pretty. Think about it, have you ever seen an ugly butterfly? What interests me is their unique beauty and stages of life, which are relatable.

STAGES OF A BUTTERFLY

1. EGG
2. CATERPILLAR
3. CHRYSALIS/PUPA/COCOON
4. BUTTERFLY

When I think of how the four stages of becoming a butterfly relate to women, this is what I gather. In stage 1, the egg is deposited. We don't know what size, shape, or color, but we will be beautiful. At stage 2, the caterpillar stage, we must get the basics, education, experiences, morals, values, and everything needed to grow and further life. At stage 3, the Chrysalis stage, although we are full grown and really don't have to prove anything to anyone, we are yet becoming. This stage can be short or take a greater length of time because we are transforming into our glamorous existence. Even in this stage, women are stunning and wrapped in silk. Stage 4 is when the butterfly emerges; this is the adult stage. As mature women, we continue to be transcendently impressive while living our best lives.

After being in one stage and outgrowing the things around us, including people, friends, etc., we tend to go into another phase of life. While going through a phase of metamorphosis/maturity; perfection can't be rushed. This stage can take days, weeks, months, or years. This is a time when we can be in a vulnerable state to others including family, significant others, associates, friends, or people we don't know. The storms that arise during this time can also affect your development just like the caterpillar becoming a butterfly. Know that working through it, to make it through it, results in a one-of-a-kind you, filled with beauty and grace. It reminds me of an old saying, "You have to crawl before you walk." Beautiful butterflies, you must crawl before you fly.

By now, you are probably wondering what makes me an expert? Well, I'm not. I'm just living and experiencing life's ups, downs, trials, errors, and happiness; and I'm still hopeful and grateful.

Here is something about me... I know the CEO of the Blessing Business! I'm told that I'm kind of a big deal to my loved ones. *Hey! Claim it and walk the walk!* Excuse me just a moment for *"My"* Praise Break!

Do you realize how many different directions you are pulled in just because you are of great value? As a woman, you are mom, many times a dad, stepmom, grandma, great-grandma, sister, auntie, wife, girlfriend, best friend, favorite cousin, sister-n-law, prayer warrior, nurse practitioner, teacher, babysitter, caregiver, chef, mechanic, top-flight security, banker, loan officer, beautician, trusted co-worker, coach, counselor, only child, eldest child, eldest daughter, baby, youngest daughter, and the list goes on and on. It's a never-ending story...

If you have at least one role in someone else's life… you are all of that and a bag of chips! Yes, I want to remind you that you too are a big deal to your loved ones. You are magnificent! I am sure that I'm not the first to tell you that; so, accept the role and embrace the blessings.

Now that we have gotten situated… let's have some fun. We can do some Q&A. This will tell you your level of glam and your age. I've been wondering… are you old enough to know about the game cake walks? What is your comfort color? Is it black, gray, or white? If so, try something new. Remember, butterflies are all colors. You will be surprised at how fabulous you look and will wonder why on earth you've been trying to hide for so long.

I know I'm not the only one, so what about you… have you ever said, "I'm going to run out, I hope I don't run into anyone who knows me?" Here you go, you are in your comfortable house clothes, maybe baggy pants, a T-shirt, and the first pair of shoes you could slip on your feet. Did I mention absolutely no makeup? Hair, no style just however it falls. In other words, you are so natural, and you think you look a hot mess! You have run your quick errand and then, suddenly, out of nowhere... someone calls your first name, or your nickname, or your professional name. OMG! You *almost* went unnoticed. It could even be someone who doesn't know your name but wants to know who you are. Wait a minute, you thought you looked your worst, but to others you were attractive. This is a Public Service Announcement, even when you think you aren't looking or at your best... you are being watched and found to be remarkable, attractive, and desirable. Here's the cherry on top, no matter your age, you are simply beautiful, embrace it!

Questions about Wonderful You

1. Do you have a favorite color? If so, what is it?
2. How do you define pretty?
3. What makes you tired?
4. What has changed about you?
5. What brings you joy?
6. Is there anything you want to change?
7. Butterfly, what stage are you currently in?
8. What encompasses your chrysalis/cocoon?

I ask these questions so that you will learn or realize something about YOU. Start and end by being true and honest to yourself. I'm not in your business… I just want you to think about your business and be honest with yourself. Okay, *I am* meddling just a lil' bit.

Here are a few fun and interesting ideas for things to do or try. Remember, keep spreading your wings and try doing different things that are outside of your box. Be willing to open your mind and heart to new prospectives and possibilities.

1. Instead of large crowds, have small intimate settings.
2. Family photo shoot.
3. Ice Cream Social.
4. Brunch.
5. Potluck with close family and friends.
6. Have a themed food night once a month.
7. Wine tasting with cheese, appetizers, etc. at home.
8. Hire a musician– pianist, saxophonist, or small band for a backyard gathering.
9. Tap into your hidden gifts and talents.
10. Walk in the park (even if it starts to rain).
11. Take a two-to-four-hour (roundtrip) train ride.
12. Dinner on a yacht.
13. Girls' morning at the spa.

14. Walk for a Cause/Cure.
15. Buy new perfume.
16. Learn to do a new puzzle. Sudoku anyone?
17. Learn a second language. Have you tried ASL (American Sign Language)?
18. Do something special or spend an hour with an elderly relative, church member, neighbor, or friend.
19. Spend quality time with your significant other.
20. Set aside time for yourself. Calgon take me away!

Here is something I purposely omitted from my list. You know butterflies love flowers. Most women love flowers. Have you or do you know of someone who has sent flowers to themselves, especially on Valentine's Day? I'm left asking, "Why?" Was it to make others look, stare, or talk?

Who are you trying to fool or impress? Questions, questions, questions... why does it matter? Why would you be concerned about what others think? If you are one who has sent flowers to yourself at work, did it truly make you happy?

I have one suggestion... *Stop It!* If you really want to feel good, get a subscription. Remember, I listed ideas to help you step outside of your box and do something different?

Here it is, yes, get a subscription. As classy and deserving as you are, don't show off or wait until Valentine's Day. Treat yourself to flowers delivered monthly. You can even feel good each day by investing weekly in a different bouquet or arrangement of flowers. This is inexpensive and can be purchased at a local supermarket, nursery, wholesale store/club, or flower shop. The exciting part is, this week you may feel like sunflowers, next week you may be feeling like a spring mix, and the following week you could feel like being exotic or showcasing quality red roses. In other words, no matter what, keep it fresh and trust that it will not go unnoticed. Move about quietly like a butterfly!

In every stage/phase of your life take a moment for YOU. If you don't like your current stage, take a break, and go into your shelter. The good thing about being a human being is you can decide to take a rest. You can go into the protective stage, go into your chrysalis or cocoon. When you go there, protect yourself, your feelings, your life and at the same time wrap up in soft silk and still shine. When you've regrouped and are ready to move forward, step out refreshed and as amazing as ever!

The last thing I will share about being born in the South, I was told, "Don't wear out your welcome." I am going to keep in line with my good home training. So, here's to you my sisters and friends... Yes, I have my hand and index finger up like they did in church as they eased out.

My 10 Things to Stay Ready

- Walk in the place like you own it... even when you don't know where you are going.
- Don't stop walking until you get there.
- Try something unique.
- Know that some people around you are working with limitations. They are giving it all they've got!
- Take a break, breathe, and just say... "Well."
- Every now and then pull rank; let them know you are the oldest. That puts "Respect" in place!
- What are you worrying about? People would love to be your size; put it on.
- On your worst day, get one of your best girlfriends and go buy a new pair of shoes.
- Always try to look a little better than you feel.

- You have to pop your gloss and stay ready for the paparazzi.

Thank you for welcoming me into your space. Take a moment to appreciate the incredible journey, and celebrate the magnificent, glamorous, and ageless girl/woman that you are!

Marian R. Featherson Bio

Marian R. G. Featherson was born in Artesia, Mississippi on Smith Oaks Plantation, a place in Columbus, Mississippi, Lowndes County. She was raised in the Midwest. Marian is married to the love of her life. They have two adult sons, an adult daughter, and Goddaughter.

She's a member of the Friendly Temple Church in St. Louis, under the leadership of Bishop Michael F. Jones Sr.; a highly recognized community and spiritual leader. Her chosen career in Management spanned over 36 years. Marian's a professionally trained model, who has blazed runways in Hollywood. Her successes also include Model Instructor, Actress, and Floral Designer.

She enjoys sports, fashion, reading, vocal music, and performance arts. Her focus is being positive, inspiring, caring, and sharing genuine love. When interacting with Marian, every now and then you will detect her Southern drawl or accent, and you will find her Southern hospitality is *always* on display. One of Marian's newest and most exciting accomplishments is being a co-author of "Ageless Glamour Girls: Reflections on Aging."

CHAPTER 12

Patricia Desamours:
A Golden Life

I recently posted a picture of my 18-year-old self on Facebook for "Throwback Thursday." It got lots of likes and positive comments, some of them from people I do not even know, but I could understand why. That picture shouts, "Joy." I had a big full-toothed smile, with my arms opened wide as if I was welcoming the world, and my chin-length hair was styled to perfectly frame my face. I had on an outfit I loved: a blue wrap skirt that showed off my waistline and a black, long-sleeved shirt with a sequined owl on the front. And, of course, I had a silky black scarf around my neck. It was the seventies, and scarves were the ultimate fashion accessory.

Just starting college, I was full of hope and dreams for a life of adventure, excitement, love, and romance. I wanted what most people want: success, fulfillment, and someone to share it all with. I thought those things would automatically come into my life once I was "worthy" of them and had proven myself to the world. Unfortunately, my definition of worthy was not something I could ever have obtained. That is because I equated my self-worth with being slim. In my mind, you could not be fat and beautiful. I had to be slim.

I grew up in a world where European beauty standards were highly prized. I can remember wanting straight blonde hair like a friend's or even curly red hair like another of my classmate's. I wanted to look like them. They were tall and slim, or athletic and freckle-faced. I was usually the only Black kid in the bunch, and I looked nothing like them. First, my hair would never fully surrender to the pressing comb. That hot steel comb, heated on the kitchen stove always brought with it burned earlobes and slightly scorched hair. It was thick and would start reverting to its natural state within hours of being pressed out slick and shiny with Blue Magic Pressing Oil. Later, when we used permanent relaxers with names like Dark and Lovely and Gentle Treatment to straighten our hair, the harsh ingredients would burn my scalp. My hair still would not stay straight for long. It was always trying to get back to its natural state. When Black Americans began embracing and celebrating their Blackness, and afros and naturals came into fashion, my hair loved it. Afro Sheen hair products made it shine. My afro was always perfectly shaped and round. I was never without my steel pick with the raised black hand for a handle to keep it picked out and fresh. To this day, an afro is my best look.

So, I did not look like any of my white friends, and I was usually the fat, "chubby" Black kid. I have been overweight, plus-sized, big-boned, or just fat for much of my life. I would guess that I have gained and lost hundreds of pounds yo-yo dieting over the decades. Diets were a way of life in my house. My mother, who was beautiful and not overweight, was always on a diet. She said that is how she maintained her size. She was disciplined about her eating habits, even though she would sometimes binge on her favorite foods. She loved potato chips and bread and desserts like peach cobbler and apple pie. But then she would make up for binging by fasting the following day or two, drinking only black coffee along with her cigarettes. And since she was always on a diet, I was always on a diet too.

AGELESS GLAMOUR GIRLS: REFLECTIONS ON AGING

My body image issues began early in life. In third grade at my elementary school, periodically, we would have to line up, get on the scales, and have our weight read out loud and recorded to make sure we were within some childhood weight and height guidelines formulated for white children's bodies. Childhood asthma kept me from taking part in P.E. or recess. Combined with my asthma medication, it was difficult to lose weight. Being weighed "out loud" was traumatic for an overweight kid who just wanted to fit in. That is when my mom put me on the Atkins diet, one of the original low-carb eating plans. I would come home from school for lunch and have a fried egg and a hamburger patty. It was protein, fats, and vegetables for every meal. I was bigger than my classmates, and it was embarrassing for my mom. Perhaps she felt it was a negative mark on her parenting skills. It was tough for me also because I was teased and made fun of. Over the years, I tried every weight loss program on the market. I tried Weight Watchers at least three times, but it never worked for me. Each time, I gained weight instead of losing it. I was traumatized all over again as an adult by having to stand in a line, step on the scales, and have someone read my weight aloud. I always felt humiliated.

A lot of my ideas about beauty came from magazines and popular culture. In the early 1960s, for young girls, Black and white, Mattel's Barbie doll was the ideal beauty, even though her measurements and figure were unrealistic. The South Shore Eating Disorders Collaborative (SSEDC) created "Get Real Barbie" to raise awareness of eating disorders related to body image and unrealistic beauty ideals seen in pop culture. The organization's fact sheet says if Barbie were a real woman, "she would be 5'9" tall, have a 39" bust, an 18" waist, 33" hips, and a size 3 shoe!". I got my first Barbie doll when I was seven years old. That was long before the toymaker included Black Barbies, so subconsciously, I was striving to create myself in the image of a white Barbie doll. I wanted those curly bangs and that long ponytail with the flip at the end. I longed for that tiny waist and flat stomach, those long, shapely legs and feet with high arches that looked great in heels. Today, of course, it makes me sad to think that I idolized a white doll who looked nothing like me and who I could never look like. It was a no-win situation.

AGELESS GLAMOUR GIRLS: REFLECTIONS ON AGING

The joy in that Throwback Thursday picture was real, but for so many years, my weight and body image issues were always in the background adding self-doubt to the equation. If I did not achieve something, I would wonder if being fat was part of the reason. For example, if I did great on the phone interview but did not get the job after the in-person interview, I thought the reason might have been because they did not want to hire a fat person. Being fat for much of my life has always colored my decision-making and my thought processes. Sometimes, I came to completely wrong conclusions about people and situations that had nothing to do with my weight. I just thought they did. My best friend forever, who has since passed away, used to shake her head at me when I would bemoan my weight issues. She would say, "Well, being fat has never stopped you from living your dreams, from what I can see." In other words, "Quit complaining!" She was right, but it took me many years to slowly figure that out. The beauty of growing older is that you do figure it out. And once I did, I grew more accepting and confident about my body. I also stopped worrying about other people's opinions about my body. That was the key to developing my self-esteem and loving and caring for myself without reservation and without that nagging voice in my head questioning my own worth.

We have all thought about what might happen if we could go back in time. I sometimes wish I could go back to the 18-year-old me in that throwback picture and reassure her that she is enough, just as she is, and her life will be golden, full of all the things she longed for at one point or another. I would also tell my younger self to stop obsessing about looks and weight and worrying about the future. It will take care of itself. I would shower her with so much love that she would have no choice but to know her worth and be confident in it. How much more might that 18-year-old have blossomed with that kind of love and encouragement. That is one reason I believe it is important, and I've made it a mission throughout my career to mentor young people, especially young Black women. There are so many intelligent, accomplished, beautiful Black women role models to learn from. But it can be life-changing to have a personal mentor who has already gone through some of the challenges you face. It is self-affirming to have a cheerleader, someone who is in your corner and whose advice you can trust and count on. I stay connected with all my mentees. It is a way of giving back. The older I become, the more important it is to me to pass on knowledge and wisdom whenever I can.

Growing older is such a deeply personal experience. When I think about how many choices you must make just in a single day, I sometimes want to map out all those past choices on a giant sheet of paper and figure out what might have happened if I had chosen differently. I was accepted to several colleges but chose a small, private Christian school close to home. I wonder how would my life have changed if I had gone to the large HBCU much further away? I was married three times and divorced three times. What if I had stayed married the first time, or the second time, or the third time? How would that have impacted my life? I like to think about these types of questions for perspective on my life today, especially when I feel as though I should be doing more or that I am missing out on life. When I stop to list all the wonderful things that have happened in my life, the wonderful people I have met and am lucky to call friends or family, that perspective helps me to be content with the choices I made in life. Even my choices that did not turn out well were like fertilizer, helping me to grow stronger and better.

For decades, I have had this thought that one day, in the future, I would be slim and fit. Well, the future is here, and I am still working on that. Even with that unfulfilled dream still tugging at me, I realize my life is truly golden. Not everyone gets a long life. To be approaching my seventh decade on this planet is a privilege and a blessing. And it is never too late to reach any goal. I know I will never be slim; that is simply not my body type. I am, however, on a journey of fitness and health that I never took the time for when I was younger. My body goals are more realistic now. The freedom that comes with age makes me sure those goals are attainable, and that is exciting. When I look in the mirror these days, I see the confident woman that time and experience have made me. Every wrinkle and every gray hair were earned, and I would not trade them for anything. I can really say I love myself unconditionally, and that is as good as gold.

I try not to offer unsolicited advice, but if I could indulge in it for a moment, I would tell you to live your life without worrying about your critics. Enjoy every minute you have because you do not know how many minutes you may have left. And when you come across a picture of your former self, celebrate that person, do not criticize. Embrace yourself, flaws and all, and know that you are precious and your life, at this moment in time, is golden.

Patricia Desamours Bio

Patricia Desamours has been writing since elementary school when a teacher assigned the class to write a book called, "Me, Myself and I." Her love of writing and reading led her to a long career in broadcast journalism. Now retired, Patricia enjoys spending time with family and friends, traveling, writing, and celebrating life. Patricia lives in metro Atlanta.

https://www.linkedin.com/in/patstclairedesamours

CHAPTER 13

Leah Irene Victoria:
Sweet Inspirations

Fashion is an expression. It has been that way with me since I was a little girl. What you're about to read has been my journey up to this point. I like to wear certain styles of clothes that keep me motivated throughout the day. I then try to pass that motivation on to others. It may be something as simple as wearing an outfit with a style and/or color scheme that gets a compliment or just simply brightens someone's day. My purpose for fashion is to promote positive vibes and bring creativity to the world.

From a young adolescent, I've always been a fan of mixing and matching apparel. I would play dress-up in my mom's closet, then look in the mirror and pretend to be someone famous. Despite my family's finances and limited resources, it never hindered my imagination or kept me from trying on clothes, jewelry, make-up, etc., that made me feel good and/or look pretty at the same time.

Attending Sunday Mass was a common tradition in my country. As a kid living in the Philippines and raised in Filipino culture, I always anticipated showcasing my dresses while walking to church. In my mind, it was like walking the runway. That childhood fulfillment received every Sunday resonates with me to this day.

My life wasn't a rainbow growing up, but I worked hard with what I had to make things a little easier along the way. True enough, today, I am at a level where I can express myself creatively and financially through fashion without any limitations. However, my purpose is not solely for my pleasure; as I mentioned, through fashion, I wish to promote positive vibes, put a smile on someone's face, and bring creativity to the world. With this fact in mind, understand that my sense of fashion does not in any way define me as egotistical or self-centered. My main goal has always been to give back or, as some would say, pay it forward!

I do this through my own foundation, where I collect nice clothing! Sometimes, the clothes are used, worn once, maybe twice, or what have you. Often, they are new or unworn items I never got around to wearing. That may sound weird, but it has become something like a Nordstrom Rack. However, some may see and interpret this negatively, which is beyond my control, but those who know me know that I have a big heart.

Of course, my lifestyle has deliberately changed throughout the years. I regularly go to the gym and attend yoga classes. Eating healthy has become a main priority in my life. I have made fish a main dish with many traditional Filipino dishes, which I include at least three days a week in my diet.

As a full-time travel nurse, I must take special care of my skin. My days are a lot different than most of my friends. First, I work overnight, and rest during the day which I believe gives me an advantage over the majority of the world, caught up in the highly stressed hustle and bustle of the daily grind. I wear the least amount of make-up when working, due to the dry and often cold temperatures of my work environment. As I have aged over the many years in this profession, I've realized how crucial it is to focus on self-care, which can add quality years to your life. My lifestyle now is a total cleansing of the unhealthy habits I used to have when it came to eating and resting. Now, I eat smarter, and rest much more than I used to. In fact, proper sleep is the true secret to feeling better and living longer. I am truly living my best life now, doing the things I love with the one I love.

Today, trends are something that we live with. Trends come and go, and many are in make-up and cosmetics. To be clear, I'm not talking about over-the-counter products, but surgeries and procedures that alter and change your make-up forever. Beauty gurus and their advice on the newest trends are some of the global authorities I rely on to keep pace with this younger generation.

Many of the products I use help maintain the elasticity of my face, allowing it to remain youthful to prolong the inevitable. Sure, I am totally aware of aging, but I think there is nothing wrong with enhancing your body, surgically or otherwise, just so long as you continue to feel confident in your own skin. Some areas of your body can get a little saggy or loose. Regenerate and rejuvenate your skin by using products that continue to make you look young and vibrant. For some of us, our dermatologist can be our best friend. Seek their advice, for they can help us live life to its fullest without needing validation from others. IT'S YOUR BODY, YOUR RULES!

Now, I focus on the one thing I can control: mentally and physically enhancing and improving myself every day. I also make sure I'm in a healthy environment, which helps preserve my peace of mind. Allowing negative people within your circle will greatly impact your natural glow. My yoga workout works as a strength and conditioning component within my routine. It is a factor in my ability to be focused and disciplined to hold myself accountable, not if - but when I slack up and get a little lazy on my journey. Indeed, your habits can be what defines you, but keeping them intact helps reflect the glow within you.

As much as we try, we can't avoid the inevitable, which is aging. As my doctor says, "Father Time is undefeated." It is human nature to age, which is life's beauty. At this point in my life, to age gracefully and live life cherishing those near and dear to me is my main goal. You can become ageless from within by teaching your mind, body, and soul to recognize toxic or mischievous personalities from outside the parameters of your circle. Your circle is your circle of life, your force field, the boundaries you have set for yourself. Protect your boundaries by keeping anyone or anything negative at bay.

Empowerment, confidence, and belief in oneself make you powerful and ageless to mankind. Becoming ageless isn't about using products, procedures, or buying things. Although some may disagree, I believe it is about doing the things you have loved throughout life, maintaining a healthy lifestyle, and having fun doing it. The bliss of what it looks and feels like to become ageless will be reflected in your appearance and soul!

In conclusion, I would like to thank my family, those who have influenced me over the years, and the experiences that have helped shape who I am as a person. These are the things that reflect in my appearance and resonate within me, giving me the bliss of what it truly looks and feels like to become ageless.

Leah Irene Victoria

World Traveler / Travel Nurse Extraordinaire

EPILOGUE

Written by Pat Battle, News Anchor/Journalist

Marqueeta Curtis-Haynes would have spotted my grandmother in any crowd - an Original Glamour Girl. She was tall and striking, strong and proud, determined and dignified. I can still recall her mantra, which no doubt set my two sisters and me on the path to what Marqueeta has most appropriately designated AGELESS GLAMOUR. We were teenagers, maybe pre-teens, while on a cherished summer visit to Jersey, our Mom, Myrtle, advised us: "Baby, never leave the house without something on your face. You never know who you might run into." Soon, mascara and lip gloss became part of our daily routines. Looking at the three of us now, I think it's safe to say we all embraced that ideal and have honored it for 50+ years. It wasn't just the lipstick or the mascara. It was everything you wore on your face: your dignity, your intelligence, your spirit, your faith - the stuff you carried to command respect. Our grandmother nearly died giving birth to our mother and her twin sister in 1932, the last of John and Myrtle Cowan's five daughters. Against all odds, she had her last child and only boy three years later. In that sweet Southern way, they just called him Brother.

We lost our remarkable mother, Glamour Girl Alma Battle, in 2010 - her story is a book. Her twin sister, Daisy, who we call Aunt Bit, is the only one of the six siblings still with us. She weaves for us the stories that are the fabric of our lives going back generations. Through this 91-year-old Ageless Glamour Girl, ageless in her own right, we visualize Myrtle Cowan's daughters crowding up to the front door of their home in Ripley just to watch their mother walk away, nudging each other gently as they took turns moving closer to the glass for a better view until she was no longer in sight. They stared at her with love and reverence as she strode off to church or a meeting, wearing grace and etiquette as naturally as the ever-present purse in the crook of her elbow. She took in sewing, worked in hotels, and like countless other women in her generation, did domestic work to earn a living. "Mama was something special," my Aunt Bit says, crying softly. "People looked at you a certain way, regarded you a certain way, and treated you as such. But most white people admired my mother; they had a lot of respect for her. They considered her part of the black upper crust, if that's what you want to call it. But she didn't have a thing! We didn't have any money. It was just the way she carried herself. She wanted to be something more." With Brother enlisted in the U.S. Air Force, two daughters married, and three in college, Myrtle Cowan went to school herself, earned a Cosmetology degree, and opened her own beauty shop in Tippah County, Mississippi - the still horribly cruel and deeply scarred South, the 1950s segregated South. Yet, she made a way, even when there was no way.

Our Mom, Myrtle, passed away at the age of 87, still glamorous! By then, I had launched my career in television news, and my incredible mother had, of course, picked up the mantle that her mother and mothers before her carried with such dignity and grace. The mantra, over time, morphed into: "Baby, don't forget your lipstick!" It was sprinkled into our daily chats before I went on the air. It was a short phrase with a far-reaching meaning: it wasn't so much about looking your best (cause sometimes we have to "make do"), but being your best self: regrouping, reinventing, re-emerging as you evolve, always representing the hopes and dreams of the generations of the phenomenal women that came before us; embracing theirs while building our own. It was learning to appreciate the gifts that God has graced each of us with and utilize them to enhance and elevate our place in the world and the lives of those around us. My grandmother planted the seeds and nurtured future generations of Ageless Glamour Girls - our daughters and cousins, their daughters. The reflections written by the women who contributed to this book are designed to encourage us, educate us, and guide us through the unavoidable aging process to navigate it with joy despite sorrows, love despite pain, and healing despite our suffering. And prayerfully, we are graced with other women who steer us gently from behind, pull us steadily from ahead, and hold our hands as they walk beside us. Ageless Glamour Girls UNITE!

JOIN

Marqueeta Curtis-Haynes:
AGELESS GLAMOUR GIRLS™

"Ageless Glamour Girls™: Reflections on Aging" is more than just a book. It's a movement, a tribute, and a testament to the indomitable spirit of women.

Join the Ageless Glamour Girls™ Movement:

Podcast: https://agelessglamourgirlspodcast.buzzsprout.com
(You can also find the podcast on your favorite podcast platform.)

Website: www.agelessglamourgirls.com

Private FB Group: The Ageless Café™
https://www.facebook.com/groups/theagelesscafe

Facebook: https://www.facebook.com/agelessglamourgirls

Instagram: @agelessglamourgirls
https://www.instagram.com/agelessglamourgirls/

YouTube: https://www.youtube.com/@agelessglamourgirls

TikTok: https://www.tiktok.com/@agelessglamourgirls

LinkedIn: www.linkedin.com/in/marqueetacurtishaynes

#agelessglamourgirls #reflectionsonaging #theagelesscafe #boldbeautifulbrilliant #healthyagingjoyfulliving #agelessaging #ageless #proaging

Thank you in advance for your support.

Printed in the USA
CPSIA information can be obtained
at www.ICGtesting.com
LVHW021452221223
767229LV00050B/936

9 781955 107440